Family Traditions in Hawai'i

Birthday, marriage, funeral and cultural customs in Hawai'i.

By Joan Clarke

Photography by Michael A. Uno

Namkoong Publishing
Honolulu, Hawai'i

First printing 1994.

Library of Congress Catalog Card Number 94-068763

ISBN 0-9643359-0-5

Namkoong Publishing
P.O. Box 61053
Honolulu, Hawai'i 96839

Printed in Hong Kong

About the cover: In old Hawai'i it was believed that *ki* or *ti* leaves would keep evil spirits away. Today in Hawai'i the ti leaf is regarded as a symbol of good luck. Salt is an agent of purification and is used to cleanse and bless in Hawaiian and Japanese traditions. In the Chinese tradition the color red symbolizes blood and the life force, possessing magical powers. It is also believed to be the color most dreaded by evil spirits thus it drives them away and is symbolic of good luck. In Hawai'i, these three symbols are an important part of rituals and customs for all ethnic groups.

Table of Contents

I was saddened to hear of my friend's mother's death. While it was expected, it was still a sad time for her and her family. I prepared a simple meal for them one night while they were in the midst of their preparations for the funeral. My husband and I made plans to attend the service.

Friends may call between 6 and 8 p.m. Cremation. So read the funeral notice in the paper. Then began the host of questions: What do I wear? Black? White? Do I give money? How much? Are flowers appropriate? How long will the service be?

We arrived at the funeral home at 6 p.m. The room was crowded with family and friends paying their respects and the smell of incense permeated the room. There was an open casket and offerings of food; Buddhist monks clad in saffron robes arrived and the chanting in a foreign language began. We sat quietly and conspicuously, not knowing what was going on or what was about to happen.

My friend and her sister were clothed in muslin-like hooded robes. They knelt, they stood,

INTRO DUC TION

they held their hands together. Their father stood nearby. About an hour later there was a pause in the chanting. We said goodbye to my friend and left, thinking that the service was over. We later discovered that the ceremony continued for another two hours, part of which included a visit to the family's temple.

This experience was the birth of the idea for this book. I was born and raised in Hawai'i and have lived here most of my life, yet there are times when I don't know quite what to do when participating in some of the celebrations and observances of life's key moments. I'm sure there are many like me. Perhaps, too, there are many like me, who question the significance of cultural customs and practices with which we have lived all our lives.

We live in a multi-cultural, multi-lingual, multi-ethnic island state which has become a melting pot of ideas and practices. Each day our lives are affected by and are a part of the cultural traditions and customs of the many ethnic groups that have migrated to Hawai'i's shores. Many of these traditions and customs have been frozen in time in our island state and maintained over many generations. Many traditions and customs have evolved over time and have adapted to a more contemporary society. But the most interesting aspect is that all of us, no matter what our ethnic heritage, participates in many of these traditions and customs as if they belonged to each of us. And they do. The blending of these traditions and customs make Hawai'i the melting pot that it is, a rich stew of Asian, European, American and Pacific heritage.

So what are these cultural traditions and customs and where did they come from? How do we observe birthdays, marriages and death in Hawai'i? What are some of the annual ethnic celebrations observed by families? How do each of us participate in and enjoy these events in a manner that shows respect and understanding? And what determines the continuation of these family traditions?

While conducting interviews and doing research, I realized that cultural traditions, very simply, survive because there are people who take the time to practice them. And the larger the ethnic population, the greater the chance of survival. A family that observes cultural traditions is more likely to do so if there are other families doing the same thing.

On O'ahu where the majority of Hawai'i's population resides, ethnic groups stage community wide celebrations and holiday observances, bringing together families and groups of families to commemorate special days and seasons with age old rituals and ceremonies. On the neighbor islands, smaller ethnic communities find it difficult to perpetuate these traditions for lack of organizational and financial resources.

Intermarriage plays a role in the survival and change in the practice of cultural customs. Families of two ethnic backgrounds are not uncommon nor are those of several ethnic heritages mixed over several generations. Families often celebrate with a mixture of ceremonies and foods reflecting their ethnic heritage. Or they may choose not to incorporate any ethnic customs at all. Racial purity within a family is a strong factor in how cultural customs are played out during life's important passages and how authentically they are observed.

Noteworthy, too, is the role of women as the proponents of cultural traditions. Since many celebrations and observances revolve around food and many women are still primarily responsible for food preparation, it is likely that traditions of the female side of the family will prevail. Further it is the women who teach children the customs. When asked whether traditions would continue in her family, one Chinese mother shook her head and commented, "Not with two sons!"

Time has diluted the importance and authenticity of many cultural customs and practices. Generations pass on their knowledge but bits and pieces get lost along the way. Why one performs a certain ritual is explained as "That's what my mother taught me to do." The significance is lost but the ritual remains over time. Eventually many customs become lost as meaning is lost.

Time is also a factor in that people sometimes just don't take the time to observe some of the age old traditions and celebrations. Even though most celebration foods can be purchased today at the neighborhood supermarket or specialty store, it still requires time to shop for it and assemble the components. Attending an ethnic festival may not be as important to a family as the Little League game or seeing a movie together. The desire to devote time to ethnicity is critical to the survival of traditions.

The desire to assimilate, to become "modern," and to Westernize has long been prevalent among many of Hawai'i's immigrant groups. Following mainstream society in its observance of life's passages is a strong desire, particularly among young and newer immigrants. Most, if not all of our observances of birth and birthdays, marriage and death are based on Western and American customs with ethnic customs as embellishment. Many third and fourth generation adults simply dismiss cultural practices as "old fashioned" or "we're American, you know."

Yet within each ethnic group there are those who want to preserve the old traditions and celebrate their ethnic uniqueness. Sometimes there is a struggle, particularly between generations, and old traditions seem to be diminishing. But there are many who are carrying on these traditions and thereby perpetuating them for future generations. And some practices are being taken up by other ethnic groups, resulting in a melting pot of traditions and customs enjoyed by everyone living in Hawai'i.

Family Traditions in Hawai'i focuses on the customs and folklore that are practiced for birthdays, marriage and death and the annual cultural traditions observed by families. They are the rituals uniquely different from the Western practices in which we all participate. Many of these cultural practices have been documented in existing literature; those discussed here were mentioned time and again by those interviewed as characteristic of a particular ethnic group.

This book is meant to be a guide for those of us who have lived here all our lives as well as newcomers to the state. It is by no means intended to be a sociological or academic study nor is it a complete reference on all ethnic and family traditions. And while a custom may be identified with one ethnic group, not all members of that group participate in these practices nor are all customs practiced in the same way. The material is presented so we can all better understand the significance of cultural traditions and customs in the lives of people living in Hawai'i. It is this melting pot of cultural traditions that makes Hawai'i a truly unique place to live.

HAWAI'I'S FAMILIES

Hawai'i, the "melting pot of the Pacific," is a virtual stew of ethnic identities, cultural traditions, folklore, customs and food that makes for an easy going, harmonious and unique lifestyle in an island state. An industrious, energetic population of immigrants has settled here, beginning with the first settlers from the Marquesas and Tahiti who became the stock of the Hawaiian race.

These early migrants maintained a cooperative society in relative isolation for over a thousand years. Captain James Cook, searching for a northern sea passage from the Pacific to the Atlantic Ocean, landed in the islands in 1778, opening the doors of international migration to Hawai'i. Western and Chinese seamen, whalers, traders and merchants followed Cook, replenishing supplies and staying among the islands' friendly people. Missionary families from America arrived in the islands in 1820, bringing with them Christian values and Western customs to Hawai'i.

In the early 1800's sugar production began in Hawai'i and with its growth came the need for labor to tend the fields. The Chinese were recruited first, then the Japanese, Koreans and Filipinos, most of whom became laborers on the plantations. Portuguese, Puerto Ricans, Scots, Germans, Swedes and a host of others also came to work in the sugar industry, adding up to over 360,000 people between 1852 to about 1930.

Life for laborers on the sugar plantations was difficult at best. They faced long days of physical labor in the fields, low pay and poor living conditions. Some found the work on the plantations too difficult or not compatible with their training. Others could not tolerate the food available in the islands. About half of the immigrants returned to their homeland. Many left the plantations as soon as their contracts ended. Those who remained in the islands established families and formed the basis of today's multi-cultural state.

Most of the early immigrants were single men who found themselves without the strong family support and network they were accustomed to in their homeland. Of those that remained in the islands, only some intermarried with women of other ethnic backgrounds. Picture brides were brought in later to stabilize the colonies of workers in the islands, reestablishing the family traditions of their homeland.

Living in ethnic camps on the plantations the immigrants observed and re-enacted the cultural traditions of their homeland, some of which have changed over time, others preserved and practiced as they had been for generations.

The Chinese, Koreans, Japanese, Portuguese and Filipinos were the largest groups of immigrants to the islands and it is their cultural traditions that are deeply embedded in contemporary Hawai'i today. There were many other ethnic groups, too, but their customs and traditions were Western in origin and were absorbed into the evolving Western society of the islands. Some

Simple wooden structures with corrugated tin roofs were typical of plantation style homes in the early 1900's. Hawai'i's Plantation Village in Waipahu recreates this era of Hawai'i's history and multicultural society.

cultural practices, too, were simply discarded.

The arrival of Pacific Islanders in the early twentieth century and the wave of Southeast Asian immigrants following the end of the Vietnam War in 1975 have added a new dimension to Hawai'i's melting pot of traditions. Immigration laws of recent years have further stimulated migration from Korea and the Philippines to Hawai'i, adding a new twist to the customs of the older immigrants who have been in Hawai'i. "Modern" immigrants today sometimes consider the older generations very old fashioned and almost foreign in the traditions that are practiced.

The following is a brief description of the family characteristics of some of Hawai'i's ethnic groups which form the basis for many family traditions.

The Hawaiian society that Captain Cook found upon his arrival was based on the ʻohana (family), a social, economic and educational unit of mutual sharing and support. The ʻohana included all blood relations who maintained a sense of shared responsibility, involvement and interdependence among its members. It is within this family structure that Hawaiian values of sharing, generosity, reciprocity and giving are taught.

Within the ʻohana, the arrival of the *hiapo* (first born child) was cause for great celebration, especially if it was a boy. Hiapo were traditionally given over to their *kupuna* (learned teacher) or grandparents, who would raise them and pass on their knowledge. And within every family a person was *punahele* (chosen) to receive the *hā* (breath), the oral history and genealogy of the family. The recipient bore the responsibility for becoming more knowledgeable and for carrying on the traditions of the family.

While the concept of ʻohana is still important in modern day Hawaiʻi, many of the traditions and rituals of daily living within the family have not continued as Western family concepts began to dominate the islands. The feasts of celebration that observed life's milestones and the rituals of living went unobserved for many generations. Some of these traditions are reappearing today among Hawaiian families.

One tradition that has maintained its importance and has been enhanced over time is that of the *hula*, the Hawaiian dance. It is a story telling tradition, a ritual of legend and history of the Hawaiian people, their lives, their places of beauty, their gods and their feelings of aloha. It is a tradition passed on through the generations that has become an integral part of island life.

Chinese immigrants to Hawai'i – 46,000 of them over a period of about fifty years – formed the backbone of the sugar plantation work force up until the turn of the century. Arriving from different clans, villages and districts in China, the early immigrants spoke different dialects and practiced different customs.

Most were migrant workers seeking to return to China with great wealth and status. Almost half of them did but many left the sugar plantations once their contracts ended to establish businesses of their own. As traders, farmers, artisans, merchants, jewelers and craftsmen, many became successful in their endeavors at the expense of being discriminated against because of their success. Second, third and fourth generation Chinese were well educated and have become prominent in all aspects of island life.

Most of the immigrants were single men and many intermarried with Hawaiian women seeking to establish the family unit that was so important to Chinese life. The family unit – father, mother, sons, daughters, paternal grandparents – was essential to life itself. The father assumed the most important role, responsible for the care of his parents and the continuity of the family name through marriage and the bearing of sons. And he was responsible for the continual worship of ancestral spirits as patriarch of the family.

The first born son assumed his father's role; sons in general were regarded as a valued asset to the family. Daughters were considered a liability for whom a dowry would have to be accumulated. Once married, a daughter left her family and became a member of her husband's family.

Chinese immigrants to Hawai'i came with a variety of religious beliefs, folk traditions and rituals that blended together to make up a folk religion of sorts. Taoism worshipped material things with imagery, symbols and superstitions. Confucianism provided a code of ethics for people to live harmoniously with one another. Buddhism provided images of a future life that was wonderful for the good and terrible for those who were not. Ancestor veneration, embedded in all three religions, firmly established the relationship between children and parents: it was a child's duty to honor his parents while they were living as well as after they died.

The Chinese in Hawai'i continue to practice many customs as insurance against the evils of the world. Their festivals, feasts of celebration and family rituals have been perpetuated over several generations in Hawai'i and will no doubt survive for generations to come.

Portuguese immigrants came to Hawai'i from Madeira and the Azores over a span of ten years, 12,000 of them hoping to fulfill their dreams of owning land and having a good job. They came as family units and they came to stay in Hawai'i with no intention of returning to their homeland. The Portuguese assimilated quickly, learned to speak English and Hawaiian, and established themselves as landholders within the community.

As laborers in the field, the Portuguese proved to be steady, conscientious workers. Many became *lunas* (supervisors) on the sugar plantations. Others brought skills from their homeland as masons, carpen-

Galos, the Portuguese rooster, is a symbol of faith, justice and good luck for many in the Portuguese community. Portuguese folklore tells of a man in Barcelos wrongly accused of crime and facing death. He pleads his innocence before a judge who is dining on a rooster. The accused man announces that the rooster will rise from the platter if he is innocent. As he says this, the rooster does rise and crow to everyone's astonishment. The man is freed and the Cock of Barcelos assumed its role as a symbol of Portugal.

ters, businessmen and plumbers and established themselves within the community. Family participation in farming, ranching and household chores took priority over educational pursuits among the early immigrants. Later generations became well educated and rose to prominence within the Hawai'i community.

Celebrations and observances of life's passages are important among Portuguese families but they are generally Western practices. Most of the early immigrants and many families today are Roman Catholic, and it is the observance of religious holidays that distinguish Portuguese family traditions in Hawai'i.

Over a thirty year period, 180,000 Japanese came to the Hawaiian Islands as part of the labor force for the sugar plantations. 8,000 Okinawans emigrated, too, and by 1896, the Japanese and Okinawans comprised the largest ethnic group in the Hawaiian Islands for the next seventy-five years.

The *issei* (first immigrants) held on to the outlook and values of their homeland, hoping to return one day with a higher standard of living. About half realized this dream. Those who stayed, men and women, worked hard and they were the first among the sugar workers to organize a labor union and a strike for higher wages. Inevitably they became prominent in the islands' labor and political scene.

Most of the Japanese and Okinawan immigrants were single men who seldom intermarried. Picture brides from their homeland helped to stabilize the life of the immigrant workers and reestablish their family units. Family and honor to the family were important to the Japanese and Okinawans who came to Hawai'i. Education was valued and many issei sacrificed years of hard work so that their *nisei* (second generation) sons and daughters could be well educated. These values continue to be important to most Japanese and Okinawan families today.

Prefectural groups called *kens* were formed to bring together those of similar origins in a social setting. An Hawaiian Japanese language developed among the different kens, cultural traditions were observed and support in time of need were offered. Today, annual picnics and events are still held with *sansei* (third generation) and *yonsei* (fourth generation) Japanese participating.

Following World War II and the discrimination they faced during this time, the Japanese tried to assimilate themselves more quickly into mainstream Western society that predominated in Hawai'i. Many cast off their old traditions and customs so they could be recognized as Americans. But the Buddhist and Shinto traditions of Hawai'i's early Japanese immigrants continue to be observed today among families and through community wide cultural festivals.

Korean immigrants began arriving in 1903, recruited by the sugar industry which sought to balance the ethnic camps on the plantations. 7,000 immigrants came over a four year period, most of whom were unmarried men with little experience in farming.

Like other immigrants they worked hard and proved to have great stamina in the fields. Many became lunas on the plantations.

Koreans assimilated into urban areas and had one of the highest rates of intermarriage among the immigrant groups. Picture brides arrived later, a strong willed group that kept alive the strong family orientation of Korean society and saw to it that their children received an education. They participated actively in religious and political events and organized financial support to help their homeland resist Japanese rule.

Korean family pride was very strong and to this day rules the Korean household. To bring dishonor or shame to the family is without question a great insult. Fathers were respected and obeyed: "I always did things to please my father," commented a second generation Korean woman. Sons, of course, were important to the continuation of the family.

Many Korean immigrants had converted to Christianity before their immigration. The immigrants came with their clergy, established churches which became not only religious and social institutions but also the foundation for anti-Japanese activity in support of their homeland. As a result of this Western Christian attitude, many of the folk traditions of old Korea were cast aside and few of the annual celebrations that were once observed like the Chinese and Japanese are seen today. With the change in immigration laws, new Korean immigrants have settled in Hawai'i. And with them have come cultural customs "new" to the old Korean community.

Filipinos comprised the last major wave of immigration to Hawai'i for the sugar plantations. By 1930, 110,000 immigrants arrived, half of whom returned to the Philippines or moved to the U.S. Mainland. The majority of Hawai'i's Filipino community comes from the Ilocos region and speak the Ilocano dialect. Those speaking Tagalog and Visayan are also among Hawai'i's Filipino community, all of whom are recognized as Filipinos, though their language, cultural practices and traditions differ.

Most of the early immigrants were male and many left behind wives and families in the Philippines. Longing for companionship, wives were later brought to Hawai'i, many of them young women who were unknowingly betrothed to older men. Early Filipino families tended to be large and closely knit. Many have sponsored other family members to emigrate to Hawai'i, continuing a tradition of support among family members.

After World War II more laborers were needed for sugar and pineapple plantations and another wave of immigrants came to Hawai'i. Many have continued to work on the plantations while many have become prominent in Hawai'i's business and political circles.

Many Hawai'i Filipinos are Roman Catholic and celebrate religious days with great fanfare and festivity, forming the basis for many of their family traditions. Beauty pageants are an important cultural tradition within the Filipino community as rites of passage and community fund raisers, further drawing together the growing community of Filipino families in Hawai'i.

Unlike the immigrants from Asia, Samoans were not recruited to Hawai'i to work on the sugar and pineapple plantations. But like the other immigrants to Hawai'i, they sought better opportunities for themselves.

The Mormon Church encouraged many Samoans to settle in Hawai'i when the Mormon Temple in Lā'ie was completed in 1919. In the 1950's, a new wave of immigrants from American Samoa came to Hawai'i, transferred with the U.S. Navy. With their families, they, like other immigrants before them, were seeking opportunities for better jobs and a better life.

The Samoan *aiga* (family) is the basic unit of Samoan society and the center of social life. The *aiga potopoto* (extended family) includes the nuclear family and its direct blood descendants and heirs and the descendants and heirs of the *matai* (family chief) who may not be related by blood. The matai leads and protects the family and its lands and arranges for members' weddings and funerals. He is entitled to loyalty, services and cooperation from the families who select him. Individual pursuits are all undertaken with the family in mind.

Next to the matai is the *tulafale* (talking chief) responsible for communicating the needs or problems affecting the community. While Samoan families have adapted to Western practices and customs, they still value and participate in the concept of the aiga potopoto in Hawai'i.

Important to Samoan tradition is that of fine mats woven of pandanus leaves, referred to as Samoan currency. The more mats a family possesses, the greater their wealth and social position. Ceremonially presented at the birth of children, weddings, the building of new houses, the dedication of a new church and at death, mats are produced by women, a craft tradition that is unfortunately waning.

The *kava* ceremony is another tradition of importance to Samoans. Gatherings that welcome visitors, the bestowing of a title of a chief and other special occasions would feature this ritual. Kava is only consumed by people of title within the Samoan community or their designees according to a formal seating and ranking order. Mythically symbolizing the creation of life from death, kava is a liquid made from the sun dried root of the kava plant (piper methysticum) that is pounded into a powder and mixed with cold water. Women traditionally prepare the kava for consumption but do not partake of it unless they hold a title.

Tongans emigrated to Hawai'i seeking better employment and education. Many, like the Samoans, were lured to the islands by the Mormon Church, the promise of employment at the Polynesian Cultural Center on O'ahu and the educational opportunities afforded at Brigham Young University at Lā'ie. Adapting to a multicultural, contemporary society, the Tongans, like the Samoans, have tried to maintain their strong extended family structure within the workings of Western culture in Hawai'i.

Handwoven pandanus mats are an important part of Tongan and Samoan observances of life's passages, valued for the time and skill of the person weaving them as well as for the quantity accumulated over one's lifetime. Finely woven mats are ritually exchanged at weddings and funerals among many Tongan and Samoan families in Hawai'i today.

Cooperation and helpfulness among members of the family is paramount to individual pursuits in traditional Tongan society. Families respect their chief and *matapule* (spokesperson), both men of honor and high status. Girls are assigned high status in Tongan families: the *mehekitanga* (father's eldest sister) is an honored position. It is she who receives the ceremonial gifts on behalf of the family at all celebrations and sees to their redistribution among the families.

Fihu (fine mats) and *tapa* (cloth made from bark) are ceremonial gifts presented at birthdays, weddings, church dedications, ceremonies bestowing titles and at funerals. Their display as decorations for a pavilion or church bestows public recognition upon women for their work. Fine mats and tapa also serve as a "red carpet" for special occasions.

Like the Samoans, Tongans have a kava ceremony, a ritual not dissimilar in its formality and hierarchy. Tongans, however, use the kava ceremony at almost all social gatherings including birthdays, weddings and funerals.

The Vietnamese

The end of the Vietnam War in 1975 and the subsequent takeover of Vietnam and Laos by Communist regimes brought forth a wave of refugee immigration to the United States. Hawai'i was one of the many resettlement camps for these political refugees and their families and the later wave of Amerasian children and their families.

The first wave of immigrants were an educated, industrious group who have become successful entrepreneurs, engineers, computer scientists and skilled workers. Later waves included "boat people" who escaped from Vietnam in search of economic opportunity in the United States. Hard working and industrious, the Vietnamese have faced language barriers, difficulty in finding housing for large families and the breakdown of traditional roles in their family structures.

The traditional Vietnamese family is much like the Chinese family. A woman marries into her husband's family, living with his parents and his siblings. The wife is responsible for the workings of the inner household, the raising of children, the preparation of meals. The husband, in his role as head of the household, provides support and protection for his family and parents, and presides over all rites of family ancestor worship.

In Hawai'i today, Vietnamese families are changing as both father and mother work outside the home in most families. There is an increasing number of intermarriages and a desire to adapt to their new environment, altering the traditional values and family ties. But filial piety and ancestor veneration are still highly esteemed in Vietnamese families owing to Confucian influences on Vietnamese culture. Buddhism, too, plays an important role in many Vietnamese families, forming the basis for many of their customs and traditions.

Because of the influence of China in Vietnam for over a thousand years, many cultural traditions, festivals and rituals mirror those of the Chinese. Western influence, notably French influence, also made its mark on Vietnamese society. With the desire to assimilate into mainstream U.S. culture and Hawaiian lifestyle, few of the old Vietnamese traditions are practiced in Hawai'i today.

The Laotian community began to establish itself in Hawai'i at the end of the Vietnam War in 1975. Government officials, the wealthy and educated came first followed by farmers, soldiers and others who escaped from Laos or were released from Communist camps. Like their Vietnamese counterparts, they have tried to assimilate into island life.

In traditional Laotian society, a young man joins his bride's family, unlike most Asian societies. Girls were valued for their capability of providing a marital alliance that would add to her family's labor force and earning power. A young couple would reside with the bride's parents, later moving out to form their own household. The youngest child, being the last one at home, would take care of his or her parents, thereby inheriting the family home and property. This traditional family structure is giving way to Western practices as the Lao people assimilate in Hawai'i.

Most Laotians are Buddhists of the Theravada school and they frequently join together in religious festivals centered around The Lao Buddhist Society Temple on O'ahu. Celebrations and observances of Buddhist holidays is prominent among the Lao community in Hawai'i.

Baci (the string tying ceremony) is a Laotian tradition performed on special occasions such as the birth of a child, marriage, the departure of a family member for school or employment, recovery from an illness or during a religious observance. Based on the belief that individuals have thirty-two souls or spirits, the baci ceremony invites these spirits back when they go wandering off. Also called *su kwon* (to invite the soul), the ceremony consists of tying cotton string around the wrist from a central ball, thus tying these wandering spirits back to the individual. This ritual symbolically bestows good luck, long life and health upon the honoree and all who participate.

Birthday celebrations are an important tradition among Hawai'i's families just as they are in the rest of America. Hardly a birthday goes by today without some recognition punctuated by birthday cards, gifts, cake and ice cream, candles and parties, all part of the American and Western traditions we live by. Whether it's a small intimate affair for just the family or a grand celebration, birthdays are considered special days for the celebrant.

Family traditions might include favorite foods for a birthday child, a day of not having to perform any chores or a special outing. Classroom parties, pool parties, a movie outing, a picnic at the park or a special dinner at a restaurant are just some of the many celebration activities of Hawai'i families. And what would a children's party be without the

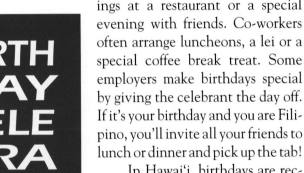

BIRTH DAY CELE BRA TIONS

"goody bag?" Filled with toys, special treats and sweets, these token gifts from the celebrant to guests is a way of saying "thank you!" for celebrating my special day.

Adults might celebrate with family gatherings at a restaurant or a special evening with friends. Co-workers often arrange luncheons, a lei or a special coffee break treat. Some employers make birthdays special by giving the celebrant the day off. If it's your birthday and you are Filipino, you'll invite all your friends to lunch or dinner and pick up the tab!

In Hawai'i, birthdays are recognized and celebrated in much the same way as they are in the rest of the United States. Sweet sixteen parties, twenty-first birthdays, and significant decade marking birthdays are all cause for celebration. But of special significance in Hawai'i are the Baby Lū'au celebrating the first birthday of a child, the Japanese Yakudoshi and sixtieth birthday celebrations.

The Baby Lū'au

The most significant birthday celebration in Hawai'i for all ethnic groups is the Baby Lū'au held in honor of the first birthday of a child. Whether it is a traditional cultural practice or a custom that has been borrowed from the Hawaiians, the Baby Lū'au has become synonymous with one year birthday celebrations.

For Hawaiians, the first birthday of the *hiapo* (first born child), particularly a male child, was very important. This child, traditionally given to his grandparents for rearing, became *punahele* (chosen), one who

Akekokula Halualani and mother, Krichelle, view the pua'a *(pig) that will be prepared for roasting in an* imu *(underground oven) in honor of Akekokula's first birthday.*

memorized the genealogical chants and assumed responsibility for the family. The first birthday of a child was also significant in days past because of high infant mortality. If a child lived to be a year old, it was, indeed, cause for celebration.

Ancient Hawaiians would celebrate this most important birthday with *'aha'aina piha makahiki* (feast of the fullness of the year). Chanting and dancing of *mele* (songs) composed in honor of the child would commemorate the occasion. Gifts of woven mats, gourds, and calabashes of poi would honor the chanters, poets and dancers who had bestowed these lifelong gifts of song and dance to the child.

Especially important to this celebration was the killing and roasting of a *pua'a* (pig), a tradition that is still practiced today among Hawaiian families. Once considered an offering to the gods, the pig and its preparation is a focal point of today's Baby Lū'au, gathering family and friends in a cooperative celebration.

The traditional Hawaiian Baby Lū'au is first and foremost a feast of food, abundant and delicious. A typical menu might include *pipi kaula* (Hawaiian beef jerky); dried *aku* (skipjack tuna); *lomi* salmon (salted salmon with tomatoes and onions); sweet potatoes; *'opihi* (limpet); *haupia* (coconut pudding); squid lū'au (taro leaves cooked with squid and coconut milk); chicken long rice; *poi*, and of course, *kālua* pig (pork roasted in an *imu* or underground oven). Tables are set and decorated with fresh ti leaves and flowers. Socializing and participation in the preparation of traditional Hawaiian foods by family and friends and the feasting, music and dance that follows, add up to a grand party celebrating an important milestone.

Baby Lū'aus are now a part of island culture. Whether its based on a traditional cultural practice or a custom borrowed from the Hawaiians, baby's first birthday is an important family affair. Small or large celebrations, prepared by family members or catered, almost every ethnic group will celebrate this important birthday in some way. The celebration may not be a lū'au in the sense of a typical Hawaiian menu but in all likelihood the fare will include a mixture of "local foods" from amongst Hawai'i's ethnic groups. No matter what the menu, food will be abundant.

Many Tongan and Samoan families would probably roast a pig for the occasion as would Filipino families, all of whom consider the pig of great importance for all feasts and celebrations. Chinese families, too, might feature a roast pig as well as noodles for long life. Red tinted hard cooked eggs and sweet pickled ginger, symbols of new birth, are sometimes served.

For Japanese in Hawai'i, mochi pounding once commemorated first birthday celebrations. The symbolic steamed rice cakes would bring good luck to the child and his family. Few families today pound their mochi, bowing to electric machines or commercially prepared mochi but it will be in evidence at a first birthday celebration.

For many Catholic Filipino families in Hawai'i, the baptism of their child is very important and it usually coincides with baby's first birthday. Several pairs of *ninangs* (godmothers) and *ninongs* (godfathers), usually close friends of the parents, are asked to participate and help to support the growth and well being of the child. A festive feast follows the baptismal ceremony.

Korean families in Hawai'i might dress their child in a traditional Korean costume for a one year celebration. Surrounded by stacks of *duk* (rice cakes) and seasonal fruits in a colorful display, the child would "choose its future" from amongst the following items, according to a custom of old Korea:

Rice, indicating there will always be food on the table.

Noodles for long life.

Dried red dates meaning many children.

Silver dollar for wealth.

Book indicating a scholar.

Pencil for a writer.

Paint brush for an artist.

Rice paddle for a cook.
Doll indicates a girl will be a good mother.
Needle and thread for a seamstress.
Hammer for a carpenter.
Small shovel for a farmer.

This custom has continued in Hawai'i today and is not unlike a Western one where it was customary to place a piece of bread, a coin and a Bible in front of a baby indicating his or her future as healthy, wealthy or wise.

In the best of island tradition, Baby Lū'aus are informal affairs where *muu muus* (loose fitting Hawaiian dresses) and aloha shirts are the order of the day. Leis, if not provided, are certainly appropriate.

Gifts for the baby, usually clothing or toys, are welcomed for this festive occasion, though monetary gifts are also appropriate. Following Chinese custom, money can be placed in red envelopes, symbolizing good luck and best wishes to the child or gifts may be wrapped in red paper.

Festivities at a Baby Lū'au include music and dance by professional troupes, family and friends strumming ukuleles and guitars, impromptu singalongs or karaoke participation for all. Games and entertainment for other young people might be part of the fun. Most importantly, a Baby Lū'au brings family and friends together for a day of celebration and fun. It is an event almost all families in Hawai'i commemorate in some way. For some it is the most important birthday celebrated. For others it is one of many birthday traditions that mark milestones in the life of an individual.

Christopher Seh-Jin Chun celebrated his first birthday, dressed in traditional Korean attire, surrounded by duk (rice cakes) and fruit. (Photo courtesy of the Chun family.)

Giving a Gift in Hawai'i

Gift giving is widely practiced in Hawai'i throughout the year for all of life's major observances: birth and birthdays, weddings, death, graduation, and retirement as well as for American and Western holidays like Christmas, Mother's Day, Father's Day and Valentine's Day. While the notion of gift giving in the islands is usually regarded as a Japanese tradition, Chinese and Koreans hold similar views which have now become a part of island tradition.

Giri is the Japanese term applied to gift giving and the idea of reciprocity or paying back what one receives. It is a moral obligation that takes the form of birthday, wedding, graduation, anniversary, and retirement gifts as well as presentations made when someone is ill or has died. Each gift of money or goods is noted upon receipt and returned in equal value at a later time. Some Japanese families actually keep a written record, assigning values to gifts and use this record for future reciprocity. Taking a gift to a party is another expression of giri, reciprocating the host's gift of hospitality. Japanese rarely go empty handed to a party hosted by any ethnic group.

Omiyage is a souvenir or item native to a particular region, hence travelers purchase omiyage for family, friends and office workers at home. One Caucasian business executive, married to an Asian woman always returns home from a business trip with a box of candy or cookies for his secretary and office staff. Not limited to people of Japanese ancestry, this idea of omiyage is well entrenched among many people in the islands.

When Japanese family members travel, the practice of *senbetsu* comes into play. Senbetsu is the gift of money to a departing traveler which is often used to purchase omiyage for the giver.

Giri, omiyage and senbetsu – the three Japanese terms associated with gift giving – are concepts similarly implanted in Chinese and Korean societies. This concept has further spread to become an Hawaiian tradition where favors are returned and business is conducted among friends. *Ho'okipa*, the Hawaiian tradition of hospitality is also a component in this idea of giving and reciprocity.

Gift giving is not without its rules in Hawai'i. Most obvious is that guests rarely show up empty handed at someone's home: flowers, a bottle of wine, a dessert, fruit or a small gift is always brought for the host or hostess.

Money is always an appropriate gift for birthdays, weddings and funerals. While many consider money vulgar or a last resort for those who lack time or imagination, it can also be a thoughtful expression. Certainly in today's society, it is a practical gesture. Monetary gifts can take the form of cash, checks, money orders, stock certificates or savings bonds. Coins and currency are sometimes fashioned into a lei, particularly for graduations or when someone is leaving the islands.

How much should a gift be? Individual circumstances, relationship to the recipient and generosity are the determining factors. For Asians, giving too much may create an obligation that can never be repaid. The generally accepted rule for calculating an amount for a birthday or wedding at which you are a guest is to estimate the cost of the meal, times it by two if you are attending with a spouse, add a little extra and round it off to a nice figure. A dinner, including beverages, that you determine to be about $20 per person would round out to at least a $50 gift.

Monetary gifts should always be enclosed in an envelope or with a card since handing cash to someone is considered crude. Red envelopes express good luck

Lisee is money wrapped in red paper or contained in red paper envelopes that is given as an expression of good wishes. Envelopes may be plain or embellished with designs or calligraphy like a greeting card. Lisee are used by the Chinese and Vietnamese in celebration of the lunar new year, given by parents, relatives and friends to unmarried children. Birthday, graduation, retirement, wedding and anniversary gifts might also be enclosed in these red envelopes. At funerals, coins are enclosed in red envelopes for those paying respects to the deceased.

indicate a long illness or hospital stay, literally being "rooted" in bed. Fruits, flowers or money are the preferred gift along with wishes for a speedy recovery.

When visiting the home of someone of Chinese background, food gifts are appropriate. Oranges, symbolizing gold and prosperity, bestow abundant happiness and are always welcome. Remember, too, the words of a Chinese woman: "Chinese can't just receive, they have to give back." If you take something to a Chinese home, you will return home with something. Take eight oranges and you will return home with three. Accepting is as important as giving an appropriate quantity and reciprocity is as much a tradition in the islands as giving.

to the recipient for a Chinese birthday, graduation or wedding.

When visiting someone who is ill and of Japanese ancestry, never take a potted plant. The roots of the growing plant symbolically

Thus it is an island tradition borrowed from the Koreans and Japanese that when you return a plate or dish that has had a gift of food, you must return it with something in it, never empty. Guests at a wedding or birthday celebration rarely go home without a small gift.

Or if you send a gift for a new child, you might receive one in return from a family of Japanese ancestry. In old Hawai'i, the gift might have been a ceramic platter or bowl to well-wishers and gift-givers. While the expense and logistics of distribution have curtailed this practice, families might enclose a gift certificate for merchandise, candy or food along with a thank you note.

Likewise, some Chinese families in Hawai'i announce a birth and acknowledge gifts with a special food package. A family might assemble red tinted hard cooked eggs and sliced sweet pickled ginger, symbols of new birth; steamed sweet buns; a slice of roast pork, and oranges representing gold or good fortune. This traditional food package would be delivered by family members to all who had sent a gift.

While this gift package remains unchanged for some Chinese families others have redefined this traditional gift, bowing to convenience and tastes. Gift certificates for roast pork, redeemable at a restaurant or shop are mailed out with thank you notes for a gift received. Or gift certificates for a box of candy or merchandise at a general store may be distributed. Taking a different form, this tradition of the Chinese birth gift still continues in Hawai'i among some families.

Practical gift givers often pool their resources with family, friends or co-workers to buy substantial gifts for a birthday celebrant, wedding couple, or new parents. Co-workers will often "pass the hat" among the office staff to collect money for a funeral observance of an associate, giving the money outright or purchasing a bouquet of flowers. While this pooling of resources may not be unique to the islands, it is certainly prevalent because of the numerous gift giving occasions that present themselves.

Floral leis are always considered an appropriate gift for happy occasions and may be given in lieu of an object or money. Even when a "no gift" rule has been established for an occasion, a lei is welcome. Birthdays, weddings, funerals, blessings, graduations, proms, business openings, retirement, victory celebrations, special dates or just to commemorate a special day are all reasons for a lei.

Floral gifts are often sent for new business openings, a custom of Chinese origin. Flowers are important because without flowers there would be no formation of fruits; without flowers there would be no success.

Perhaps the most important adult birthday is when a person attains the status of "adult" at the age of twenty-one. Twenty-first birthday celebrations are usually focused around the fact that a person has attained the legal age to consume alcoholic beverages and as such it is a rite of passage that usually means a night on the town with friends.

For some the twenty-first birthday holds greater significance. For Tongan and Samoan families, the twenty-first birthday is ceremonially marked with the presentation of "the key of life" from father to child. Symbolic of the freedom of the new adult, especially for girls, this ritual is accompanied by the presentation of mats and cloth and a kava ceremony.

Passage into adulthood in Laotian society means that a young man becomes a novice in the Buddhist temple for a period of time. At about the age of eighteen he shaves his head, dons the robes of monks and lives in the temple. Not only is it a form of training for the young man but it also earns merit for his parents who have raised him. Living within the temple for a few days, a week, a month or longer, some young Laotian men in Hawai'i observe this tradition of their religious background.

For girls, eighteen used to be a time when "coming out" parties were held, introducing young ladies to society and a host of young men. While debutante balls or "coming out" parties are not prevalent in Hawai'i, some Filipino families honor their daughters with a grand party that spotlights their beauty and youth.

As one gets older, specific birthdays take on great significance among Hawai'i's Japanese, Korean and Chinese families.

The Japanese and Okinawan Yakudoshi

The red envelope arrives in the mail with the red-on-white printed invitation to a forty-first birthday party. But you had just celebrated your friend's fortieth birthday a year earlier. Must you celebrate another birthday? Absolutely! It's your friend's *yakudoshi* and you're about to share in all the misfortune of this significant birthday.

According to Shinto tradition, there were certain climacteric or bad luck years in a person's life which the Japanese call yakudoshi. *Yaku* means calamity, *doshi* means years, thus the years in a person's life when bad luck or disaster will strike.

The forty-second year for a man and the thirty-third year for a woman, based on a lunar calendar, are considered the worst years and are called *daiyakudoshi* or the great calamity years. (According to the lunar calendar, a person is a year old at birth, thus on a Western calendar these would translate to a person's forty-first and thirty-second years.) The Japanese written character for forty-two can be read as *shi-ni* or "to death"; thirty-three can be read as *san zan* or "misery." Thus disaster could result in these years so care and caution are to be exercised. No new projects or changes in lifestyle are recommended.

According to Japanese tradition, visiting a Shinto shrine to petition the *kami* (spirit) for blessings at this dangerous time is one of many practices that could help to dispel the bad luck of these years. In Hawai'i, the most popular practice is to have a party with family and friends so that they may share in the celebrant's bad luck. This party is referred to as The Yakudoshi. It can be a small family affair at home or restaurant or a large celebration at a teahouse or hotel banquet room. Observances are traditionally on the day of the birthday but not before and are usually grander for men than for women.

At Yakudoshi parties for forty-one year old men in Hawai'i there is usually an abundance of food and drink, symbolically sharing the bad luck of the celebrant with guests. Family and friends "roast" the honoree and duly note his accomplishments and deeds to date. The honoree usually wears a red shirt and a red lei, red being the color for good luck.

Symbolic decorations seen at most Japanese celebrations would be prominent at a Yakudoshi as table and cake decorations and favors. These would include:

Cranes, believed to live 1,000 years, thus they symbolize a long and noble life.

The turtle, said to live 10,000 years, symbolizes longevity and endurance.

Bamboo symbolizes longevity, endurance and resiliency.

Pine, revered as the home of Shinto gods, is symbolic of vitality and of strength and courage.

Lobster, whose bent body signifies old age, symbolizes a youthful spirit and longevity.

Kasane mochi, a stacked centerpiece of pink mochi atop white mochi, is symbolic of good luck and purity.

Special foods at a Yakudoshi celebration would include:

Tai (red sea bream), a favorite fish in Japan because its name is also the last syllable of the word *omedetai* meaning happy and festive. Tai is traditionally presented whole because to cut it would be to cut up the happiness and good luck it represents. *Ahi* (yellow fin tuna) or *aku* (skipjack tuna), are sometimes substituted because of their red color.

Sekihan, a dish of red azuki beans and rice is traditionally served for good health and to drive away evil spirits.

Allen Kajioka sports a red chanchanko *(sleeveless jacket) and* boshi *(cap), the traditional attire for the celebration of his* kanreki *(60th birthday).*

Mochi, steamed glutinous rice cakes, symbolize longevity, unity and strength.

B a n z a i   t o a s t s, shouted three times in unison by the guests to the honoree would be led by a respected older person. The honoree and family would shout banzai to the guests, returning the wish "may you live 10,000 years."

Gifts for a yakudoshi celebration run the gamut from funny to practical. Family and friends often pool funds to buy a set of golf clubs or other item of significance to the celebrant. Monetary gifts are appropriate and given according to your relationship to the honoree.

Among the Asian communities in Hawai'i, only the Japanese and Okinawans choose to celebrate this climacteric event. Approaching his fortieth birthday, a fourth generation Japanese man had to decide which birthday to celebrate: his American side said to celebrate his fortieth, his Japanese side said his forty-first. Of course, he celebrated both.

The Sixtieth Birthday and Beyond

In the lunar calendar, the passage of each of the five elements – wood, fire, earth, metal and water – with each of twelve animal years makes up a sixty year or sexagenary cycle. The sixty-first birthday (sixtieth on a Western calendar) marks the beginning of an individual's second childhood. It is an important event for many Chinese, Japanese, Okinawan and Korean families in Hawai'i, often commemorated with a large party or family gathering.

While this is considered a yakudoshi, Japanese and Okinawans call this celebration *kanreki*, *kan* meaning cycle, *reki* signifying calendar. Since a person symbolically enters his or her second childhood, Hawai'i celebrants dress as *akachan* (infant) sporting a *chanchanko* (sleeveless jacket) and a *boshi* (a circular beanie-like cap). The customs, foods and symbols for a forty-first birthday celebration apply to the sixtieth birthday since it is also considered a climacteric event in a person's life.

Koreans call the sixtieth birthday celebration *han-gap*. As with other Asian groups in Hawai'i, the children of the celebrant often give the party in honor of their parents.

Chinese celebrate the sixtieth birthday, too, usually with a banquet that would include long life noodles. Families might also serve a large steamed bun filled with little sweet steamed buns. A dramatic presentation for the celebrant, the large outer bun is opened revealing its contents of little buns which are distributed to family members, bestowing good luck upon the recipient.

Among Asians in days past, living to be fifty-one was regarded as the ordinary limit of life. Sixty-one was a remarkable feat and seventy used to be considered "the rarely reached age" and was cause for great celebration.

Double numbers used to be significant, too. Seventy-seven is known as the age of joy. The character for rice in Japanese can also be read as eighty-eight, hence the rice celebration at age eighty-eight. A few Okinawan families in Hawai'i celebrate the rice year with a *Tokachi* celebration, usually on the eighth of August. Feasting on pork dishes, sekihan and other traditional foods is accompanied by traditional folk music and dance.

Tokachi is a bamboo stick with a diagonally cut end used to level the rice being measured in a square box. An essential tool to rice measurement, the tokachi came to mean "may you always have an abundance of rice" and it became symbolic of one's eighty-eighth birth year. A tokachi celebration would have on display a large basket heaped with rice and tokachi whose flat ends are painted red for good luck.

Many Filipino families in Hawai'i like to honor a retiring parent, usually on his or her sixty-fifth birthday. The combination birthday and retirement celebration is, in the Filipino tradition, a festive and fun filled feast accompanied by lots of music and dance.

Not all of these birthdays are significant for every family in Hawai'i. But many children choose to observe these milestones to honor their parents, grandparents and other family members, hosting events to commemorate the occasion and observe traditions of the past.

In Hawai'i weddings are conducted throughout the year in churches, temples, shrines and other sacred grounds. They are staged in homes, at scenic spots, restaurants, hotels, private clubs and other venues of the couple's choosing. Wedding ceremonies and celebrations are as simple or elaborate as one prefers and can afford and they are quite traditional in terms of American and Western customs. The bride wears white, rings are exchanged, there's cake cutting, garter and bouquet tossing rituals. But island weddings today are embellished with a host of charming customs and rituals that are unique to weddings in Hawai'i.

Marriage ceremonies in Hawai'i vary from informal to formal, determined by one's religious affiliation or lack thereof. Christian liturgies, Protestant and Roman Catholic, Buddhist ceremonies, Shinto rites and weddings by justices of the peace are the most common forms of rituals.

Christian ceremonies of marriage are usually held in a church. The exchange of vows and rings, prayers and blessings constitute the traditional

MARRIAGE CUSTOMS

ceremony.

Weddings in the Buddhist tradition are less structured primarily because these ceremonies are a recent phenomenon. Buddhism, more concerned with proper action and one's afterlife, did not celebrate marriage in a formal way. Sects, such as the Jodo-Shin, became popular among many people and developed wedding ceremonies so that they could officiate in all of their members' rites of passage. Buddhist ceremonies are generally short and some are patterned after a Christian ceremony.

Shinto wedding rites follow the pattern of all Shinto ceremonies: purification, offerings, chanting and the sacred feast. In the feast, the bride and groom sip *sake* (rice wine) in front of the altar. *San san kuro* (three-three-nine) refers to this ceremony where the groom and bride pass successively larger sake cups and sip sake three times from each cup. Three times three is considered a lucky combination and is symbolic of tying the bond together for life.

Non-denominational marriage ceremonies are performed by justices of the peace or other persons legally entrusted to perform such rites. These traditional and non-traditional ceremonies can include personally written vows, poetry, and music which the bride and groom have chosen. Ceremonies might be held in lush garden settings, on a mountaintop, at the beach or in other venues. Underwater ceremonies complete with scuba gear and favorite holes at a golf course have also been the scene of nuptial vows.

It is curious to note that few people attend wedding ceremonies in Hawai'i, choosing to attend the celebration only. "It's bizarre," said one Christian minister. "There's no one in the church for the ceremony. People here don't attend the wedding. On the mainland you don't go to

the party unless you go to the ceremony."

The reason? Shinto ceremonies have always been a family only affair. Formal Buddhist ceremonies are a recent phenomenon and were usually for the couple only. Morning ceremonies followed by evening receptions may make it inconvenient to attend both. Some families may be preparing the wedding feast, usually a feat of great proportions involving every able family member. Some people just want to party and not be bothered with the serious side of the day. Whatever the reason, there will always be more people at the wedding reception than the wedding ceremony in Hawai'i.

Korean wedding ducks are a traditional gift presented to the bridal couple by family or close friends. The male duck sports the color blue, the female wears red. Ducks are always bound to their spouses, no matter how far away they travel thus they symbolize the unity of the couple. When displayed together in the home, the ducks indicate marital harmony.

It's the wedding feast in Hawai'i that is so telling about ethnic diversity in Hawai'i. Where else in the world could you find a single buffet table laden with *sushi, chow mein,* roast pig, *lumpia, kim chee,* roast beef, ham, rice and potato-macaroni salad? Or where in the world would a Chinese banquet be more popular than a Western buffet?

Ethnic foods are almost always at a wedding celebration with no set pattern or set menu for each ethnic group. Koreans will usually have *kim chee* (spicy pickled cabbage), *yak bap* (steamed rice confection) and various kinds of *duk* (rice cakes). At a Vietnamese party one might encounter a dish of chopped chili peppers on the table and *chagio* (fried spring rolls). *Lechon* (roast pig), *lumpia* (Filipino spring rolls) and *pansit* (noodles) might be in evidence at a Filipino wedding. Laotians like to serve *laap* (highly seasoned beef) for good luck. Traditional *kālua* pig might highlight a Hawaiian wedding celebration.

Chinese will serve long life noodles as a wish for longevity for the married couple. Shark's fin or birds' nest soup are often served because of their delicacy and rarity. Oysters are served for good luck, good things and prosperity. *Kau yuk* (red pot roast pork) is served with steamed buns symbolizing good luck because of its red color and prosperity because of its fat. Because it is fat and lean it represents the fat and lean years of life. A sweet and sour dish would be included to represent the wish for lots of children.

In fact, a Chinese banquet of seven or nine courses is the most popular wedding feast at restaurant and hotel banquet facilities among many ethnic groups in Hawai'i. Following Chinese tradition, planners will choose an odd number of courses because odd numbers cannot be divided evenly therefore it represents strength. Nine courses are preferred because nine, the largest of the single digit odd numbers stands for long, old and ethereal, symbolically meaning the couple will live together forever. Five courses would never be served because it is the number served at a funeral banquet according to Chinese tradition.

Chinese banquets are a serve yourself affair except that Chinese custom dictates that you serve others first, thus everyone serves each other. Noodles are never cut during cooking or serving; doing so would be bad luck. Serving sizes must be watched because everyone at the table should have an equal portion.

Chinese banquets, even though the hosts are not Chinese, will usually feature a bottle of Scotch on each table of ten, accompanied by a bucket of ice. It's a help yourself affair and a jigger of Scotch is used to toast each course as it arrives, adding to the festivity of the wedding celebration.

Bowing to the demands of a busy society, few wedding feasts are staged in the home with food prepared by the family. Occasionally among Hawaiian, Samoan, Tongan and Filipino families whose strong network brings together many hands to help, a wedding celebration might be a family affair. Most families in Hawai'i today prefer to let someone else do the work of cooking, serving and cleaning up.

Of special note during island wedding feasts: guests will often tap their glasses with their silverware as a signal to the couple that they must kiss. The origin of this custom remains unexplained but it is practiced at almost all island weddings, not once, but many times throughout the celebration.

Wedding Toasts

Wedding celebrations generally close the formal program with a toast to the bride and groom, wishing them happiness and a bright future. In Hawaii it is no different except the usual "Hip, hip, hooray!" or "To your health!" is often expressed in different words.

Portuguese exclaim "Salud!" meaning to your health.

Chinese say "Gonbei," and Koreans say "Mansei," both meaning may you live 10,000 years. Filipinos shout "Mabuhay" for long life to the couple. Each is usually repeated three times.

"Banzai" the Japanese version of the same word is traditionally offered three times as a toast at weddings and celebrations, first from the guests to the couple then returned from the families of the couple to the guests. Curiously, "banzai" was used in Japan to show respect for the Emperor and was repeated three times with raised arms and hands. "Kampai," meaning "here's to your health" is the traditional toast used in Japan for weddings and other celebrations and is finding favor in Hawaii today.

Old China had many rituals and ceremonies for marriage that were very detailed and clearly laid out. A matchmaker selected a bride for a prospective groom and the almanac would be consulted to determine if the match would work and to set a propitious wedding date. Agreed upon gifts would be exchanged between the two families. The bride, dressed in red, would be transported to her new home where one of her first duties was to pour tea for her new in-laws as a sign of honor and respect.

While these old rituals are not formally engaged in today, glimpses of them are seen in Hawaiʻi, particularly if two Chinese families are being united. Once engaged, the family of the groom might send a whole roast pig and wedding cakes to the bride and her family, checking first to be sure it will be happily accepted. Wedding cakes are sent in even numbers like 200 or 400, some of which are returned to the groom's family, according to tradition, along with the head and tail of the pig. In return the bride's family might choose to send the groom-to-be a new suit of clothes. This exchange of gifts once formalized the betrothal of the couple.

Margaret Dang poured tea for her parents May Har and Yau Sam Tan, observing an old Chinese wedding custom. According to Chinese tradition, the tea table is decorated with pomelos and sweetmeats. And traditionally, the pourer always uses both hands to pour and to present the tea.

A bridegroom might enlist his friends to help him carry off the bride-to-be from her family home, reenacting the bridal procession in automobiles rather than the palanquins of old. One prospective groom was turned away three times when he called for his bride, another custom of the past.

While not universal or obvious to all who attend a Chinese wedding, the tea ceremony is perhaps the most prevalent of the traditional Chinese wedding customs seen today. The bride may change from her white wedding gown into a red *cheong sam* (fitted, high-collared Chinese dress) and serve tea to the groom's parents as well as her own.

Tea is a beverage integral to Chinese life and

drinking it is a celebration of life. Tea is offered with honor and respect by the bride to her new in-laws. It is, of course, to the bride's advantage to pour tea, according to a Chinese matron. In return for this display of respect and honor, she will receive jade or gold jewelry from her mother-in-law. Lisee would also be given to the bride by every family member she serves.

The order of pouring tea follows Chinese tradition: the groom's paternal grandparents first, followed by maternal grandparents, father, mother, uncles, aunts, brothers, sisters-in-law, then sisters. Men always come first in the pecking order. The bride's parents might also be included today in the tea pouring ceremony, again following the male first ranking order and following the groom's parents. Each family member who receives tea is expected to give a gift of jewelry or money wrapped in red paper.

The tea ceremony is generally a private affair for family only, held in a small banquet room of a hotel or in a family home. The bride's

The Chinese lion prances and dances to the sound of drums, cymbals and gongs, chasing away evil spirits at weddings and other cultural celebrations. The Cantonese lion costume is the most colorful of the Chinese lions. It is the only one with a mirror that aids in chasing away evil spirits and a horn that symbolizes wisdom and superhuman powers. A Taoist ritual is performed to bless a new lion and to give it "life." Only when this ceremony is complete can the lion be played and danced and perform its duty of chasing away evil spirits.

maid of honor is usually on hand to assist. On a few occasions the tea ceremony may extend to all who attend the wedding reception, in which case all present must be prepared with two lisee for the bride with at least a dollar bill in each envelope. Red envelopes are sometimes provided for the occasion.

As guests are seated at a Chinese wedding banquet, an announcement will be made and the sound of 10,000 firecrackers, popping in the distance will be heard, warding off evil spirits. One or two hotels in Honolulu have come to take this literally: instead of the real thing, a tape recording of the sound of firecrackers is played.

Following the noise of the fireworks would be the noise announcing the arrival of the Chinese lion and his entourage. Again a way of warding off evil demons on this most auspicious day, the lion dances through the banquet hall, receiving dollar bills from guests through its mouth opening. It is hoped that the more money given, the more the giver will receive back one day.

The most distinctive feature one might see at a Japanese or Okinawan wedding celebration is the display of 1,001 *origami* (folded paper) cranes. These paper *tsuru* (cranes) may be hung from bamboo poles or displayed as a framed art piece in the shape of a bird, swan, carp, happiness character or *mon* (family crest).

The bride traditionally folds all the cranes, symbolically displaying her patience. Today she will usually enlist the assistance of her bridal party, friends and relatives in the task of folding them or she may purchase pre-folded cranes. According to local custom, the bride must fold at least one herself for good luck.

At some Japanese weddings,

A traditional decoration at a Japanese wedding in Hawai'i is the display of 1,001 cranes. Cranes are believed to live 1,000 years and thus symbolize a long and noble life.

a whole red fish would symbolically bestow good fortune and happiness upon the couple. The *tai* (sea bream) is preferred though another red fish might be used. It is traditionally displayed with a "fish net" of carved turnip, and vegetables carved into the shape of a crane or turtle. This symbolic fish might also be employed by a prospective groom to formalize a betrothal, a custom that was once widely practiced in the islands.

Okinawan wedding receptions will sometimes end with the *kachashi* dance, an impromptu dance in which guests perform a segment in turn. This lively and improvisational dance is characteristic of many Okinawan celebrations.

Money dance is the first thing that comes to mind when you ask anyone about a Filipino wedding: bride and groom dance to a favorite popular tune or Filipino love song while guests place dollar bills in the mouth of the bride. Hardly sanitary but very traditional at many island Filipino weddings.

Bitor, the showering of the wedding couple with money was a custom of the past that measured the prestige of a family in the community. A plate would be placed in the middle of the banquet hall and guests would toss coins into the plate. Or in exchange for a glass of wine, guests would offer money gifts and place them in a plate. The coins would be gathered up into a handkerchief and given to the groom who would then pass it on to the bride, the household treasurer.

Benjamin and Dina Castillo pass money between their teeth, performing the traditional money dance seen at many island Filipino weddings.

The pinning of money gifts to the clothing of the bride and groom as they danced to folk music is a variation of this custom. A further variation that is prominent today in Hawai'i is the placing of money into the mouth of the bride while the couple dances.

The money dance has become a tradition at almost all island Filipino weddings. Attendants stand nearby to collect the gifts of currency, usually in $1, $5 or $10 denominations. Sometimes the money is placed in a small envelope then into the mouth of the bride. A lei of money placed upon the bride and groom might begin the festivities.

Traditional Protestant and Catholic marriage ceremonies predominate among island Filipino families. Part of the ceremony might include the tying of a white cord around the bride and groom, symbolically binding the couple together. Coins are presented by *ninang* and *ninong* (female and male godparents), representing a sharing of wealth. Sometimes old, these coins are to be kept by the couple and passed on to their children. Candles light the path of the newlyweds.

Filipino weddings in Hawai'i feature a great number of ninang and ninong, sponsors for the bride and groom. Ten to fifteen pairs or more may be seated at special tables and recognized for their role in the lives of the bride and groom. They are honored guests and sometimes help in the details of staging the wedding celebration including some of the expenses.

A Filipino wedding would not be complete without joyful and festive music and dancing that characterizes most Filipino celebrations. "Singing and dancing are a must," according to a Filipino man, especially to celebrate a happy occasion.

Samoan families are an extended network of relationships that form a cohesive, cooperative society. Marriage is the bond of two families and according to *Fa'a Samoa*, the old Samoan way, marriages were arranged, particularly among prominent families. Prominence was measured not just by monetary wealth but by the power, authority and prestige of a family. Marriage was a way of maintaining one's position in Samoan society.

The importance of marriage begins with the arrangements and preparations for the celebration itself. Extended families would prepare the roasted pigs, taro, and yams to be laid out on tables for guests. Gifts would be accumulated, to be exchanged on the wedding day. *Toga*, gifts presented by the wife's family to the husband's family, consisted of fine mats, tapa cloth, fans, coconut oil, sleeping mats, and combs.

Oloa are the gifts presented to the wife's family from the groom's family, traditionally consisting of pigs, chickens, boats, houses, land, shells, tools, nets, clubs, spears and other implements. Over time, oloa has changed to become monetary gifts, placing value upon the gifts that have been presented by the bride's family.

Once all the gifts are ceremonially presented and received with speeches and fanfare by the *tulafale* (talking chief), the groom might present gifts to other chiefs present. What was left over was divided in half for the bride's family and the groom's family who all shared in the gifts that were given. In Fa'a Samoa, all members of the families shared in the wealth and prosperity of the uniting of two families, receiving back what was given.

Following the wedding, the mother of the bride might present her best store of finely woven mats to the wedded couple as their wedding bed. These precious mats represent the preciousness of the bride and are reciprocated by the groom and his family with gifts of money and food.

Today in Hawai'i, some of these Samoan traditions have continued as they have for generations. While arranged marriages are not as prevalent, a few are still discussed by fathers of young adults and family chiefs. Most Samoan weddings take place in a Christian church followed by a celebration feast, usually prepared by members of the extended family.

The tradition of the exchange of gifts between two families is still carried on today by some Samoan families in Hawai'i. While some prefer to pool their resources and just have a party in which everyone can share in the joy of the day, the Samoan tradition of sharing among the family prevails. Fine mats may not be as available today as in years past but they still retain great value and esteem in the lives of the Samoan community.

Tongan society is based on an extended family that is extremely important to individual identity, social relationships and the functioning of the community in general. Marriage is a permanent bond of families that results in sharing and lifelong support within the family system.

Marriage celebrations are a big event among the many Tongan families in Hawai'i. Great effort goes into the preparation of food by members of the extended family for the extended family, friends and church members. The roasting of a pig in an underground oven is customary; taro, sweet potatoes, corned beef and other foods would be prepared and laid out on banquet tables.

The bride and groom might wear the traditional *ta'ovala* (waist mat) that is traditional for Tongan ceremonies. The mats for this occasion are usually white and finely woven, attesting to the importance of this celebration.

Still an important tradition of a Tongan wedding in Hawai'i today is the gifting of fine mats and tapa made by women and the preparations of food by men for the feast table. These offerings of *koloa* (treasures) are made throughout the wedding feast by the bride's family and the groom's family.

The *matapule* (chief's spokesperson) announces the gifts of mats, tapa and food on behalf of the bride's family to the groom's family. The *mehekitanga*, oldest sister of the groom's father, receives the gifts from the bride's family and likewise the bride's mehekitanga receives gifts from the groom's family. The bride and groom retain a portion of these treasured gifts and the remainder is returned to the members of both families. Baskets of leftover food are often taken home by all guests.

Gifts from the bride's family to the groom's family are as large as can be amassed. The more lavish the presentation the better, for it's a mother's way of saying how good and precious her daughter is. Koloa is not just a matter of material goods being exchanged but represents the social relationship of two families and the production of goods among family members. Koloa represents family honor and wealth through valuable social relationships that are priceless.

49

Dignitaries, representatives of noble families, the church minister or a person dancing at the marriage celebration may also receive gifts of mats or cloth from the host family.

Also important to the wedding celebration is the kava ceremony, a ritual that occurs at almost every Tongan gathering. What is special on this day is that the bride is allowed to sit in the place of honor and receives the first cup of kava served by her husband. Only on this day is a woman so honored in the kava ritual.

Within the small Laotian community, wedding celebrations are a festive affair in which bride and groom don the traditional and elaborately woven clothing of their homeland and participate in age old rituals to insure their happiness and prosperity.

One of the folk practices seen in Hawai'i is that of bargaining between bride and groom. With a sense of humor, the groom must first prove himself to the bride and her relations at the wedding celebration. Entering the audience of family and friends, the groom is asked what his intentions are and what he has to show for himself. Bantering between the groom's supporters and the bride's entourage ensues and the groom offers gifts to win the favor of his bride. After the lively bargaining, the groom crosses over to the bride's side but not before his feet are washed by a young girl in an act of purification.

Baci (string ceremony) is a ritual characteristic of most Laotian festivities that would be carried out at a wedding celebration. Bride and groom will be the first to have their wrists tied with string, symbolically inviting their wandering spirits to return and enhance their future lives together.

Bride and groom will publicly pay their respects to their parents, thanking them for their support and love and asking for their blessings and advice. Gifts of silver or money will be given to the couple from their parents. This display of respect is not uncommon at gatherings of Laotian families.

Friends may call from 6 to 9 p.m., service 7:30 p.m. Or call from 8:30 to 10:30 a.m. Mass. Burial to follow. Grave side service. Private services. Cremation. Service over ashes. Inurnment. Taoist service. Memorial service. Casual attire. Aloha attire. No flowers.

These notes from a day's obituary notices in the newspaper reflect the variety of observances and practices for the deceased in Hawai'i. Just as we commemorate other passages in life, ceremonies at death provide a focus and a way for survivors to gather and recall the life of the deceased. These rituals help survivors to grieve and accept the reality of death.

Funeral and memorial services can take place in a church, temple or shrine, in a home or backyard, at the beach or on a mountaintop, on a boat or at a funeral home or mortuary. Most funeral services in Hawai'i are based on religious beliefs that dictate the general structure of the ceremony and how a person is to be buried. The wishes of the deceased expressed prior to death, family preferences and economic realities become decisive factors in making funeral arrangements.

It is sometimes difficult to distinguish cultural practices from religious ones, particularly among Asian ethnic groups where religious beliefs and practices became such an integral part of everyday life and thought. Confucian philosophy, Shinto festivals, Taoist ritual, Buddhist practices and ancestor veneration all contribute to cultural lifestyles. Add on Christian values and Western conduct and the result is a conglomeration of traditions, customs, and practices that are observed at funerals in a variety of ways.

There are a multitude of cultural practices prevalent among families of an ethnic background that relate to death. Members of an ethnic group may observe all the cultural practices documented here or none at all. Those discussed here are those mentioned most by individuals who have observed funeral customs as practitioners and participants in life's final rite of passage.

FUNERAL TRADITIONS

Ask a funeral director about a funeral for an Hawaiian person and without exception they characterize it as a party. Certainly not that death is a happy occasion. On the contrary, death is a sad time, and Hawaiian families observe death with solemn rituals which honor the deceased and enable the living to accept death. It is a time for friends and relatives to gather together to express their closeness and unity.

'Aha'aina make (funeral feast) was a tradition of old Hawai'i held to comfort mourners. This custom continues today and it is a time to reminisce about the deceased, to celebrate the individual's life and to celebrate life itself. While sadness prevails, a party-like atmosphere sweetens the sorrow of the day. "We have parties to let the dead go, so we can get on with our lives," stated an Hawaiian woman. "We mourn. Once it's *pau* (finished), it's pau."

Most Hawaiian funeral services today are Christian or non-denominational. A wake is usually held the night before the funeral service, either at the church or the funeral home. Music, often with the accompaniment of ukuleles and guitars, is in keeping with Hawaiian traditions. Floral leis to drape over the casket are often brought by mourners as well as monetary gifts for the family. Family members will be dressed in black or white.

Hawaiians generally prefer burials to cremation, possibly because of old beliefs that held bones to be symbols of immortality. As such, *iwi* (bones) were guarded, respected and treasured by relatives. The ultimate insult would be to burn the bones of a deceased person.

Mourning after death and at the funeral may take the form of requests, bequests and scoldings according to customs of the past. If you had some kind of *pilikia* (trouble of any kind) with the deceased, it is important to go to the funeral to take care of the problem. The deceased might be asked to give in to a long standing dispute or scolded by a fishing partner for going away. It is believed that the spirit of the deceased is nearby but must be told to go away so that the living can live. This "talking to the dead" is a private ritual still practiced today by some individuals.

Favorite things of the deceased are often placed in the coffin based on a belief that these items are needed by the spirit in the next world and would hasten his departure. It is also believed that if the spirit sees old things around, it will likely return and bring sickness into the household. The sight of the deceased's things would further bring sadness into the family and thus they are buried to signify the reality of separation.

At the funeral, it is believed that if a coffin

seems especially heavy to the pallbearers, it is because the deceased is not ready to depart or is unhappy with the funeral arrangements.

Salt is important as a purifying agent. *Pī kai* (ceremonial sprinkling of salt water) is a custom still practiced today by some families. Salt water is used to purify oneself upon returning home and is sprinkled throughout the house, driving out bad spirits after there has been a death. *Kapu kai*, ceremonial bathing in the sea, purified an individual after coming into contact with a corpse

Funerals mourn and celebrate the passage of life; cultural customs insure that the proper rituals are performed for the deceased.

and is another custom practiced by some today. Hawaiian salt might be thrown into the hearse and ti leaf bundles attached to the door handles for good luck.

Funeral directors report the reappearance of koa caskets at Hawaiian funerals today, hand built by families who have gathered this prized wood for this purpose. *Tapa* (cloth made from bark) and *lau hala* (woven pandanus), once used to wrap the deceased for burial, have been used to rebury bones that have been unearthed at burial sites. In remote areas of Hawai'i where mortuary services are not readily available, salt has been used to preserve the corpse until mortuary arrangements are made.

Chanting, once a major part of Hawaiian funerals is making a reappearance today. This chanting took the form of a genealogy stating who the deceased was, who the person married, who the children were and what the deceased did in life. This oral tradition firmly implanted the deceased in the memories of the mourners and provided the basis for a common bond with the deceased.

Many funeral practices of old Hawai'i have disappeared as Western practices dominated the islands. A few continue in remote areas of Hawai'i and some are reappearing with the resurrgence of interest in things Hawaiian.

Funeral customs of the Chinese date back thousands of years, many of which are still practiced and adhered to today by some families in Hawai'i. These practices draw from Taoist rituals, Confucian ideals, Buddhist thought and ancestor veneration. Taoism provides the basis for many of the practices seen at a funeral for someone of Chinese ancestry, though not all funeral services for Chinese are Taoist. These funeral customs take precedence over religious beliefs and the combination of several religious rituals within a funeral is not unusual.

It is important to note that most Chinese today – third, fourth and fifth generation in Hawai'i –are Christian who follow the rituals of their church. In reading obituary notices it is usually among first, second and third generation Chinese whose services are listed as Taoist or Chinese. A fourth generation Chinese woman simply explained, "I just did what the priest told me to do, just like the rest of the family. I don't know the rituals but it was my grandmother's funeral and that's what she wanted."

The following are some of the customs and beliefs that Chinese families observe that are most commonly seen today at funerals for someone of Chinese ancestry.

The custom of giving lisee and a piece of hard candy to all who attend the funeral is observed by many Chinese families in Hawai'i. Lisee, red paper wrapped money, usually a nickel or dime at a funeral, is given to bestow good luck and good fortune upon the recipient. The money is supposed to be spent on a sweet treat that day. The hard candy is unwrapped and eaten during the funeral service, symbolically sweetening the sorrow and sadness of the day.

Lisee and candy are distributed upon arrival at the funeral service and at the time of departure from the grave site. Pallbearers and helpers are generally given lisee of $1 to $5. The family of the deceased must insure that there is a sufficient supply of lisee and candy for all who attend the funeral. Some mortuaries provide prewrapped lisee for their clients.

Folk wisdom among Chinese dictates that you turn away when the coffin is being closed or lowered into the grave. Funeral directors announce the event. It is believed that by turning away, the spirit of the deceased will not see who is confining the body to the coffin or committing it to the ground. Illness and misfortune might befall the person who was recognized, particularly if the age of the person was in conflict with that of the deceased as determined by the Taoist priest. It is also believed that the soul of a living person could be captured by the deceased and sealed in the casket if one did not turn away.

A funerary banquet is generally held following the burial service, usually at a Chinese restaurant. This tradition dates back to old China where villages were far apart and people traveled long distances to pay their last respects. A meal would be served as a token of appreciation. A rice bowl filled with food and a pair of chopsticks would send the travelers back to their home. The tradition of the funerary banquet is still practiced but the rice bowl and chopsticks is not as commonly seen today in Hawai'i.

Considered the mecca of ancestor worship for the Chinese community in Hawai'i, Mānoa Chinese Cemetery on O'ahu is the "pulse of the watchful dragon of the valley." It meets all the Chinese standards for a burial site: sloping hills with mountains to the rear, open fields to the front, a body of water flowing nearby, and a pleasant ambience for a peaceful resting place. According to tradition, tombstones face north. These characteristics of a cemetery are also valued by Korean and Vietnamese families according to their cultural traditions.

Traditional funerary banquets consist of five courses of simple, mildly seasoned foods. According to old tradition the food would be vegetarian. Jai, a vegetarian dish, is sometimes eaten the night before or the morning of a funeral by the family. It is sometimes included in a funerary banquet today along with chicken, fish, roast pork, salted eggs, and tofu.

Chinese generally bury the deceased though some, particularly Buddhists, prefer cremation. Female family members will usually dress in white and males in dark colors. Black arm bands and bows are often worn by family members for most funeral ceremonies among Chinese families.

At the funeral of a child, one might not see parents present as dictated by Chinese tradition. Parents cannot bury their children, no matter what their age. The eldest brother of the child's father (uncle) would assume the responsibility for the child's funeral.

Many Chinese will engage in folk practices to ward off evil spirits that may be present at the time of a death. When a family member dies, the family might turn on all the lights in the house and cover pictures with white paper or turn them front side back. Red decorations in the house would be removed.

Upon returning home from a funeral, some Chinese will light a fire of newspaper or dried leaves and walk over it to keep away evil spirits. "I always have a bowl of water with pomelo leaves at the doorstep and we always wash our face and eyes when we come home from a funeral," said one Chinese woman. Both rituals purified individuals after attending a funeral.

"We had to tuck a piece of green onion in our blouse. It was wrapped in plastic. I don't know what it was for," said one Chinese woman. Regarded as a device of protection, the green onion was once used to make a tea if someone felt ill or faint from the grieving, wailing and sadness of the day.

The family of the deceased might observe a period of mourning that could last up to a month. Family members do not visit friends because doing so would be visiting your grief upon another household. Solemn activity, no jewelry or makeup are customary practices. "When my grandfather died, we weren't allowed to go anywhere for a month," recalled a woman from Hilo. "As children, we thought this was a punishment. We couldn't go to the movies, we had to stay home."

On the doorway of the house, families will sometimes hang black paper with characters announcing that there has been a death in the household.

Many of these practices prevail in Hawai'i today though not all families or individuals observe them. Those that observe the folklore and customs associated with death are doing so as they have been observed for centuries.

Attending a Chinese/Taoist Funeral Service

Within the Chinese community in Hawai'i, Taoist or Chinese funeral services occur occasionally for first, second and third generation Chinese. These services are conducted according to the presiding priest and are based on rituals that open the way into the next world assuring comfort and prosperity for the deceased. Services are sometimes referred to as "Chinese traditional;" some may have Buddhist and/or Christian traditions intermingled.

The priest determines the time and date of the funeral based on the time and date that the deceased was born and died. The priest will also determine the birth year of people whose destinies would be affected by attending the funeral and post a notice at the entrance of the funeral chapel. Those who believed this would pay their respects to the family and leave the service. Menstruating or pregnant women are also not allowed at a Taoist funeral.

Upon arrival, visitors receive a piece of wrapped hard candy to be eaten upon receipt to sweeten the sorrow of death. Lisee, usually a nickel or dime in red paper, is also distributed to be spent that day on something sweet.

Scrolls decorate the funeral chapel and an open coffin is placed with the feet of the deceased facing the door of the chapel, allowing for the soul to depart. Male family members seated to the right of the coffin would be dressed in dark clothing with black arm bands on their left arm. Female family members, seated to the left of the coffin, would wear white and have a black bow pinned over their right breast.

The oldest son sits nearest the head of the coffin, followed by brothers, sons-in-law and grandsons. A widow, daughters-in-law, daughters and granddaughters, oldest to youngest, take a secondary position to the oldest son and his descendants according to Chinese custom.

Deceased women are dressed in an even number of pieces of clothing, men in an odd number. Additional clothing may be placed in the coffin for burial, ensuring that the deceased would have clothing in the next world. In the embalming process, a silver coin might be placed in the mouth of a man and a pearl in the mouth of a woman, providing protection for the body from decay and to light the path for the soul into the next world.

Beneath the coffin might be lighted oil lamps to provide light for the soul. Longevity couplets might be placed on the body. Incense, candles, tea, wine, and food are offered. A bowl of rice with chopsticks inserted vertically will be prominent. During the service, the rice will be transferred to a crock by the priest and each family member will add rice and liquor for the departed soul. The crock will be taken to the cemetery for burial in a special niche at the foot of the grave.

The priest infuses vital power to paper images which are burned in special receptacles, transmitting this power into the next world for the comfort of the deceased. Paper offerings often include a house, a boat, a car, "servants" to lead the way and a trunk for carrying the deceased's possessions.

Representations of gold and silver ingots and funerary money are burned so that the deceased will have money to pay debts, buy services and accumulate merits in the afterlife. The more "money" burned by family members, the better the deceased will be in the next world.

The service itself consists of chanting and the offering of prayers by the priest so that the road may be opened for the departed soul. Sounds from a bell, drum, clarinet or cymbal might be heard amidst the burning of incense, candles and paper money.

Visitors paying their respects would enter the chapel, approach the coffin and respectfully offer a bow. Those believing in Taoist ritual would bow three times with hands together, light three sticks of incense and offer a prayer. All visitors would circle the coffin counterclockwise, paying respects to members of the family seated around the coffin.

Visitors are expected to stay for the duration of the service which usually lasts about two hours. During this time *dim sum* (steamed dumplings) might be served. At the end of the service, visitors would walk around the coffin for a final viewing, followed by the family. White gloved pallbearers transfer the coffin to the funeral hearse for transport to the cemetery. Along the way, water soluble paper money is scattered along the road to pacify evil spirits that might be following the procession. But holes in the paper money make it difficult for spirits to follow since they have to go through each hole.

At the grave site there will be more offerings of burning incense and candles. Food offerings of five vessels each would be laid out along with wine, rice and five pairs of chopsticks. The number five represents the five elements: fire, wood, metal, earth and water. Customary food offerings include a whole chicken with head and feet, a whole fish, tofu, prawns and roast pork.

The priest chants and makes offerings, calling the soul to accompany the body into the grave. As the coffin is lowered, flowers are removed and family members will turn away. Uncooked grains of rice and the pallbearers' gloves are tossed into the grave. Firecrackers are lit to ward off evil spirits. Visitors are again given a piece of candy and lisee.

Most families will observe a mourning period of a month during which time it is believed that the spirit soul of the deceased returns home for a visit with the family. Sometimes families choose to end the period of mourning immediately after burial, performing another ceremony at the grave site. When this ceremony is over, sons are given a flashlight and their wives are given a flashlight and a comb. The flashlight is to provide light on the way home; the comb symbolically means that the sons will branch off like a tree and the family will flourish.

When a spouse dies, the living spouse breaks the comb in half and places it in the casket, retaining the other half as a remembrance. All members of the family are given a sprig of juniper or evergreen tied with a red ribbon and lisee. The burning of firecrackers concludes the ceremony.

For families of Japanese and Okinawan ancestry, funeral observances are a time of bonding through common grief. It is considered important to attend the funeral of a family member or a friend and it is also a time to fulfill obligations. Attendance and absences are duly noted. Promptness is important and unless otherwise specified, black or dark blue clothing is the norm. On the neighbor islands, suits are still the code of dress for funerals. Monetary gifts are customary for Japanese funerals.

Services vary but are generally Buddhist or Christian with Shinto ceremonies occurring occasionally. Many of the customs observed within the Japanese community are based on Buddhist traditions and many of those discussed here would apply only to those families subscribing to the Buddhist faith.

In earlier times, the family of the deceased would be responsible for preparation of the body for burial. *Yukan*, a ceremonial washing of the body, was performed by family members who then clothed and prepared the body for viewing. This practice occurs occasionally today but in a symbolic way. Family members might convene at the mortuary along with the Buddhist minister. The body of the deceased is covered in a white sheet and the family members pour warm water over the body from the chest down.

Before the days of embalming, the body would be laid out in the yard and the family would maintain a vigil throughout the night, protecting the corpse from animals and recalling the deceased person's life. This was the original wake which today has come to mean an evening service at the mortuary or sometimes at the home. Wake services allow for the full viewing of the deceased before it is cremated. While few families conduct a wake at home, a few may, particularly if the deceased had been in a hospital or rest home. As people have become busier, wake services have diminished in favor of a wake and funeral service combined or just a funeral service.

In days past, following the cremation of the deceased, the family, led by the father or oldest son, would go to the crematorium. With chopsticks in hand, the father or eldest son would pick up the remaining bones and pass them on to the next family member until they had made a complete round of the family. The bones, along with the ashes, would be placed in an urn and taken home. While this tradition is rarely seen today, it is still considered bad manners to pass food from chopstick to chopstick, since it is symbolic of the bone ceremony at death.

Funeral services are conducted before or after cremation. If the body has already been cremated, photographs of the deceased person are commonly displayed, some professionally taken long before death to insure a nice portrait at the funeral.

Families subscribing to the Buddhist tradition will observe a forty-nine day period of mourning following the funeral, traditionally known as *shojingyo*. Literally meaning "right effort" or proper form of mourning, this period meant you were to abstain from social activities and observe a solemn period of respect for the deceased. The eating of vegetarian foods and abstinence from animal foods was considered proper for this period and was observed for forty-nine days. Food served following a funeral service used to be vegetarian. Today, food served after a funeral for family and close friends may be vegetarian but meats are also included. The period of shojin has also been shortened, usually to seven days, and some families have done away with it altogether.

In death, Japanese and Okinawan families observe that opposites apply. The number of ingredients in the dishes served and the number of dishes served after a funeral must be even, contrary to the everyday practice of odd numbers of ingredients and dishes. *Musubi* (rice balls) are shaped round for a funeral as opposed to triangular in everyday preparation. If the deceased is dressed in a kimono, the opening is crossed right over left. Tea is poured backwards from a teapot, thus one would never pour tea in this fashion in normal times.

During the traditional Buddhist forty-nine day mourning period, it is believed that the spirit is present or around the home. Candles are burned continuously at the family's altar in the home, providing light for the spirit. A service would be conducted on the forty-ninth day.

But if the forty-ninth day falls in the third month after death, the service is held on the thirty-fifth day. In Japanese, the third month is *mi* (third) *tsuki* (month). But it could also mean dissolving into nothingness, an undesirable meaning when concerned with the spirit of the dead. So the end of shojin would occur on the thirty-fifth day in the second month after death.

A few families still observe that there are certain days when a funeral cannot be held called *tomobiki* days. Tomobiki means to pull with you and it implies that the dead will take another family member or friend with them. Occurring every six days, the bad luck of these days is counteracted by the placement of six earthen dolls in the coffin to satisfy the god of death.

Upon returning home from a funeral, many Japanese throw salt over their shoulder to purify themselves before entering the house. Families might keep a salt shaker handy in the garage just for this purpose, warding off evil spirits and purifying themselves after a funeral.

In Hawai'i Japanese immigrants banded together to form a support group known as *kumiai* or *ku*. These neighborhood groups came to the assistance of the bereaved family and helped with the funeral arrangements and logistics. Members of the kumiai would stay in the family home to keep watch or they would prepare food to be served following the funeral. Others would receive the koden as mourners arrived and record the gifts. A kumiai member would usually be the master of ceremonies for the Buddhist service. Transportation would be arranged for by the kumiai so that all could attend the services. Annual gatherings of kumiai members would be held and nominal dues collected for the group's activities. Today, kumiai still exist among the Japanese and Okinawan communities, attracting younger people and members of other ethnic groups. Kumiais organized by street block seem to be forming and social activities are part of the attraction for younger members.

Those families following Buddhist traditions would be reminded by their temples of memorial services at one, three, seven, thirteen, seventeen, twenty-five, thirty-three, thirty-seven and fifty years. Family participation in these memorials are considered very important.

A fourth generation Japanese man attended the observance of his paternal grandfather's fiftieth anniversary of death, dutifully paying respects to a family member he had never known. Asked whether he would observe these same rituals for his parents, this man said yes, because it was important to his parents.

A Caucasian man married to a Japanese woman reported that at an observance of his mother-in-law's anniversary of death, family members traveled form the mainland to attend even though they had not attended the funeral years before. For some families, these observances are as important as the services at death.

Money and Flowers for Funerals

Monetary gifts for funerals are referred to as *koden* by the Japanese and they have been credited with this practice that has become widespread for all ethnic groups in Hawai'i. Crisp new bills are placed in a clean white envelope and given to the deceased's family to help defray the expenses of the funeral. A supply of these envelopes is routinely available at the reception area of the funeral home.

Koden actually means "this is for your incense expenses." This became stylized to represent money for the funeral expenses. It has been a long standing practice of Japanese society and it was an important custom when immigrants working on the sugar plantations had little money for funerals. Giving money for a funeral is now customary for almost all ethnic groups in Hawai'i with the exception of Caucasians. "I tell haole families not to be offended," said one funeral director of the custom of giving money at funerals. "Everyone does it and it's very practical."

The amount of money given depends on how close you are to the deceased and your relationship. Within Japanese families, the amount of the koden is also determined by how much the mourner or his family had previously received from the family of the deceased. Giving back koden of equal value represents an obligation fulfilled; new obligations are created when koden is given for the first time. Families sometimes keep a record which is used for future reciprocity at funerals.

Giving money to the family of the deceased is widespread in the islands for all ethnic groups. $10 or $20 is a customary amount but there are wide variations depending on your relationship to the deceased. Cash or checks are placed in envelopes or with a card of sympathy.

During the plantation days, Japanese families acknowledged the attendance and gifts of mourners with a small gift. Tins of coffee were often distributed on Maui; tea was traditionally given in Japan. Gifts are not in evidence today though mourners might be handed a thank you card immediately upon giving their envelope.

Flowers given for a Japanese, Okinawan, Chinese or Korean funeral should be white or yellow and always without thorns. A second generation Korean woman recalled: "When my father passed away, we wanted red roses. So we had them, a gorgeous wreath of red roses. But we were scolded so much afterwards because it was a thorny flower." White and yellow chrysanthemums are preferred for a funeral for island Asian families.

Family requests regarding flowers, usually listed in the obituary notice, should be followed. An abundance of floral arrangements may mean an additional expense for the family in moving them from mortuary to grave site.

Ancestor worship, Confucian philosophy and Buddhism all had a strong influence on Korean society and cultural practices evolved along the lines of those in China and Japan. But Christianity was warmly embraced by the Korean nation and many immigrants to Hawai'i were already converted when they arrived in the islands. Many funeral services in Hawai'i are Christian, dictated by the family's church affiliation; Buddhist services are also prevalent.

Only a few traditional funeral practices are evident today in Hawai'i. Foremost is that Korean women still wear white clothing for funerals, the symbolic color for death in Asia. "From the time I was a little girl, I always wore white to a funeral. So I always wear white today; it doesn't feel right to wear anything else," states a second generation Korean woman. Men usually dress in black.

Wailing by women was once a normal part of a Korean funeral. It gradually disappeared, but has reappeared at services among newly arrived immigrant families from Korea where the practice has continued.

Koreans usually prefer burial to cremation, depending upon their religious beliefs. Sometimes the deceased is dressed in traditional Korean clothing for burial.

A photograph of the deceased with a black ribbon over it may be displayed next to the casket. It might be carried by the oldest son or daughter preceding the coffin as it leaves the church or funeral home. This custom, often seen in Korea, is said to be a throwback to the time when Japan occupied Korea. Funerals for Japanese military officials usually displayed a photograph of the deceased with a black ribbon. This practice was later incorporated into Korean funerals and is sometimes observed in Hawai'i.

While attending a Korean funeral, it would not be unusual to be served food during the visitation period preceding the funeral service, usually coffee and pastries. A banquet, usually of Korean food, is served after the service, offered by children in a display of respect and piety for their parents.

Not unlike the Chinese, Koreans choose their grave sites carefully, preferring hills surrounding a sloping area and a body of water upon which to look out. And like the Japanese and other Asians, monetary gifts in a white envelope are customary for the family of the deceased.

Attending a Buddhist Service

There are numerous Buddhist sects in Hawai'i, each with its own rituals and customs for funerals which have evolved over time. There is no prescribed order of service which can be applied to all Buddhist sects just as there are no set arrangements for Christian services.

Among the most prevalent of Buddhist sects in Hawai'i is the Pure Land or Jodo Shin whose funeral services have been standardized throughout the state and generally follow a prescribed order. The ringing of temple bells and the entrance of the minister begin the ceremonies. A master of ceremonies, usually a family member or close friend, opens the service and provides a brief history of the deceased person.

Chanting begins and the immediate family begins the ritual of offering incense. A symbol of purification, incense is a kind of perfume that dispels odors, hence it dispels anything evil or undesirable. In the Jodo Shin tradition, powdered incense is offered, a pinch taken with the right hand and placed over sticks that have been lit and laid down in a burner.

As incense is offered, a person places the palms of their hands at chest level and bows deeply. This is accompanied by the Nembutsu or recitation of the name of Amida Buddha. Following the family and close relatives, members or representatives of various organizations in which the deceased was a member and members of the congregation are called upon to offer incense. More readings, a short sermon and a hymn would follow. Eulogies and condolences are offered by speakers and a message of appreciation from the family is given. The Nembutsu is repeated and the service ends.

Buddhist services are held in a temple or at a mortuary with rituals and practices varying from sect to sect. The offering of incense and the chanting of sutras are common to most Buddhist services which are generally an hour long though some may be longer. Following the service, the casket is taken to the crematorium though some services may be conducted following cremation.

When attending a Buddhist service, one would sit and observe the rituals. Participation in the offering of incense is up to the individual. Respects would be paid to the family prior to the start of the service.

Important to the Jodo Shin tradition is the post funeral memorial services. The first is observed by family members the day after the funeral. Six days later, then every seven days thereafter up until the forty-ninth day, a memorial is observed at the temple or in the family home. Memorials at one, three, seven, thirteen, seventeen, twenty-five, thirty-three, thirty-seven and fifty years are also observed.

Buddhist services within other sects and among other ethnic groups vary widely but will include the chanting of sutras and the burning of incense. The forty-nine day mourning period is important to all Buddhist sects as are the memorial services years later.

Filipinos in Hawai'i are generally Christian, mostly Roman Catholic, and the traditions of their churches will determine the kind of funeral service to be held. Cultural practices and folk traditions, however, play a role in a Filipino family's observance of death. Filipino customs, transported to Hawai'i from specific villages in the Philippines may have different meanings for families from different villages. For purposes of discussion here, the practices mentioned by participants and practitioners will be grouped as Filipino though it should not be implied that all Filipinos share in these beliefs nor do all Filipinos engage in these practices.

With roots in ancestor worship, many Filipinos view death as the passing from one realm of existence to another. There is great concern over the soul of the deceased and many practices revolve around the belief that proper care must be taken to assure the soul's final journey.

As soon as a person dies, all the windows in the house might be opened in the belief that it would allow the soul of the deceased to depart. The family might set a log afire in the front yard to keep away bad spirits and it is watched by family members and friends. If any firewood is stolen, it is believed that someone else in the household will follow the deceased soon. The fire is kept burning until the deceased's body is returned to the house or the family returns from the funeral, a period of many days.

Some Filipino families like having the deceased brought home for one last stay, a practice that is diminishing. At home, the casket is placed in such a way that the feet of the deceased faces the front door to allow the spirit to depart easily. Folk wisdom says that the living should not sleep in this position.

If the casket is brought home it is critical that it not touch the door jambs of the house. It is believed that spirits reside in door jambs and should not be disturbed. Some Filipinos say that a casket can only leave the house through a window so that the spirit will not return. By leaving through a doorway, there would soon be another death in the household. A window would stop the close interval of deaths in the family.

One funeral director recalled a scene at a Filipino home: "They insisted the body had to go out the window of the house. Well, the coffin was too large. So they got a chainsaw out and made the opening bigger. I've seen some families demolish a house to get a coffin out!"

Old time funeral directors have reported that in days past when the casket was leaving the house, a member of the family would cut off the head of a chicken and throw it at the feet of the funeral director. Slaughtering an animal was believed to help the deceased go to heaven. "I've had Filipino families throw a ceramic dish at my feet as I left the house," recalled a Hilo funeral director. "The crashing noise was supposed to chase away the evils spirits, I guess."

Following a funeral, many Catholic Filipinos observe a *novena*, nine nights of prayer for the deceased. Sometimes the funeral is held on the ninth night or the novena will begin on the night of the funeral. It is believed that on the fourth or ninth day, the soul of the deceased would return. Food is left on an altar in the home or on the steps of the house for the spirit to consume.

During these nine nights, prayers are offered for the deceased by friends and relatives who bring food and socialize. Card games, mah jong and other games of chance are usually a part of the socializing that occurs during this mourning period. It is believed that the merriment brings about a joyful atmosphere for the deceased's journey into the next world. On the ninth night a feast is given in honor of the deceased.

Filipinos generally bury their deceased in mahogany or dark wood coffins which are usually packed with lots of clothing and personal articles. "When my father died, we packed his clothes, his favorite hat, wristwatch, wallet, eyeglasses, dentures, tweezers, sakura cards and family pictures. He was dressed in a *barong* shirt. If you don't put these things in the coffin, the deceased will return for them," explained a Filipino woman.

Candles for light, needle and thread, shaving kits, cigarettes, many changes of clothing and all manner of personal effects are placed in the coffin, under and around the body for the spirit's journey into the next world. Shoes are usually left off the deceased but placed inside the coffin. If the spirit returns, the family does not want to hear it walking around. Jewelry might be placed on the body for the funeral service but removed before burial to lighten the load into the next world. Some believe that jewels and shoes damn the deceased to hell.

Upon leaving the church family members might pass under the coffin being held high by the pallbearers. Doing this would enable the family to face the reality of death by forgetting the deceased and overcome their fear of spirits that may return during the novena nights. Some believe that this act would help the family avoid illness or great calamities.

Emotional displays of grief and wailing are not uncommon at Filipino funerals. Nor should one be surprised to see photographing and videotaping of a funeral. Sometimes these visuals are sent to the deceased's family in the Philippines or displayed in the family home following the funeral.

The family usually dresses in black with many women wearing a traditional black veil. Widows often wear black for up to a year after death and children might wear a black pin. Flowers are welcomed as are monetary gifts to the family.

When a family returns home from the funeral, they might walk over the burning log in the yard so that spirits will not follow or cause illness or another death in the family. Ashes will be thrown on their shoes symbolically dispersing the evil spirits. A tub of water mixed with lemon grass, lemon leaves, guava leaves or vinegar is available at the doorway for all to wash their face and neck in a purification act.

Stopping somewhere like the grocery store on the way home from a funeral is a custom one Filipino woman also practiced to distract evil spirits from following the family home. Family, friends and relatives might go to a river or to the ocean on the day following a funeral to ritually wash away the grief of death.

Following the ninth night of prayer or after a forty day mourning period, a feast is prepared and served at the family home or the funeral home. It is believed that such a feast must be lavish so that the deceased will be honored and the family's prestige will be increased. If the deceased's spirit is not content with the festivities, family and friends could suffer misfortune. It is also considered a time for those who have been unfriendly to the deceased to restore friendship and avoid a hostile spirit in the future.

Attending a Christian Funeral

Christian funeral services are generally simple and constant. While there is no specific order or program for services among the many denominations and churches, most services will follow a general pattern. There is usually a visitation period prior to the formal service during which friends may pay their respects to the deceased and the family.

The service itself consists of readings from the Bible, prayers, a sermon and the singing of hymns by individuals or the entire congregation. Clergy speak of the deceased person and a close friend or relative might offer a eulogy.

Services are usually held at a church, the funeral home or at the grave site. Caskets may be open or closed, the body may be buried or cremated, all according to the wishes of the family. The family will also determine, through the obituary notice, the attire for attendees, the desire for flowers or their omission, and whether or not charitable donations are to be made. Gifts to the family, if any, would be determined by cultural practice.

Roman Catholic services might follow more formal rituals including the Mass of Christian Burial. Services are generally in a church with a prayer service or wake occurring the evening before.

Catholics generally follow the custom of body burial. Though the Catholic Church does not forbid cremation, the Church does not allow ashes to be brought into the church for a funeral mass. Cultural preferences have allowed for a dispensation, however, in Hawai'i, and a mass may be said over the ashes of the deceased.

Paying one's respects at a Christian service is a simple and straightforward affair. Pausing at the casket or urn, one offers a prayer or observes a moment of silence, then offers condolences to the surviving family who is usually seated in the first row or pew. Following the service, one may proceed to the grave site where a brief service follows.

Samoan families follow a number of different Christian denominations; many belong to the Mormon Church. Families and friends would dress up for a funeral, a sign of respect for the deceased; Mormon families usually dress in white. Cremation among Samoans is rare and if it is done, there is no interment of ashes. Music and song characterize Samoan funerals, seen as a comforting gesture to families.

Samoans will line the grave site with mats and tapa avoiding burial directly in the ground. In old Samoa, people, objects or anything of importance are generally never placed upon bare earth, a bare table or directly on the floor. A liner or mat would always cover the surface. Many families construct wood or concrete liners for the grave site in keeping with this cultural practice.

The burial of fine mats and tapa with the deceased is sometimes lamented particularly in a time when the production of these items is on the decline. Great value is placed on these mats and the presentation of mats and tapa at a funeral is a cultural tradition that continues today in Hawai'i. Gifts of cloth, scented oils, flowers and money are also seen at Samoan funerals in Hawai'i.

Following burial, a feast is held consisting of pork, beef, taro, yams and other staple foods of the Samoan diet. Several funeral directors recalled the custom of the distribution of slices of pork at a Samoan funeral. Appearing to be raw, the pork would be cut on the site following the service and handed out as mourners left for home. While this practice is not commonly seen today, food baskets may be distributed to those attending the services.

Samoan families often pay tribute to their loved ones with structures at the grave site. Houses, awnings, fences, and markers are decorated and tended with care.

Tongan funeral services in Hawai'i are usually Christian and are held at the deceased's family church or sometimes at a mortuary. They are characterized by lots of singing by the church choir during the service. At one church where Tongans worship, church members will sing through the night prior to the day of the funeral, a way of comforting the family and sharing in their grief.

The church or funeral home would be decorated with fine mats and tapa by members of the family. Usually part of the deceased's *koloa* (treasure) that has been accumulated in life, the fine mats and tapa are hung on the walls and laid on the floors providing a beautiful visual display of craftsmanship that honors the deceased.

Some Tongan families follow cultural tradition and use tapa as the first layer of clothing for the body of the deceased. A *ta'ovala* (waist mat) might be used to dress the deceased. The open casket is usually placed on layers of fine mats on the floor of the church or funeral home and family members will encircle the casket. Fine mats are also used to line the grave site and the coffin is lowered upon the mats for burial.

The ceremonial gifting of fine mats and tapa occurs at funerals as it does in all important occasions in Tongan life. The greater the presentation, the more respect and esteem is bestowed upon the deceased. Bolts of fabric may also be offered in lieu of fine mats and tapa whose production is decreasing with time.

Other gifts of flowers, scented oils, bread, meat and other food are laid before the coffin and ceremonially received by the *matapule* (orator) of the family who assumes the responsibility for all arrangements. As with other Tongan occasions, there is a redistribution of gifts and the matapule organizes the presentation of food made from the family to the mourners at the end of the day. Baskets of pork, yam, taro, bananas and other foods are presented to departing mourners to take home rather than to be eaten on the premises.

While some Vietnamese are Christian, the majority of Vietnamese in Hawai'i are Buddhists of the Mahayana school whose funeral services are characterized with chanting, incense offerings and prayers. Ancestor veneration also plays an important role in Vietnamese culture as seen in the funeral and post funeral observances.

Family and friends will gather at the mortuary for the services. Offerings of food are placed at the foot of the open casket, burning incense fills the air and the sound of chanting by the monks and members of the temple is heard. It is believed that the more chanting there is, the faster the spirit of the deceased will reach heaven.

Family members are dressed in white and black clothing. They may don muslin-like hooded robes made especially for the occasion, a practice of the past that was once also common at Chinese funerals. They will kneel, bow and pray for the souls of the deceased, based upon their heritage of ancestor veneration and Buddhism.

Vietnamese Buddhists observe the seven day and forty-nine day rituals of most Buddhist sects. On every anniversary of death, the family would perform a ritual at the temple, offering food and incense to the spirit of the deceased.

Like the Chinese and perhaps due to their influence in Vietnam, Vietnamese prefer cemetery sites that are sloped and surrounded by mountains. Family ancestral plots would house the remains of generations of a family.

Today in Hawai'i, many families cremate the deceased following the funeral services for a very practical reason: deep down, many Vietnamese would like to be buried in their family plot in their homeland. Transporting ashes is much more practical given the time it may take to realize this dream and the cost considerations. While awaiting this return to the homeland, ashes are kept at the family's temple; food offerings, incense, candles and prayers are offered at regular intervals in keeping with their beliefs in ancestor veneration.

Most Laotian families in Hawai'i believe in the Theravada school of Buddhist doctrine and the rituals and practices at death are reflective of their religious beliefs.

Soon after death, Buddhist monks will visit the deceased's home to tell the deceased that he no longer belongs to the house, an expression of the finality of death. This also protects other members of the house from bad spirits. A white string is tied around the house, signifying death and keeping spirits away.

In keeping with Buddhist tradition, male members of a family, especially the oldest son, might become a monk for a day or longer when the father of the family dies. The men will shave their heads, offer prayers and meditate with the monks for a few days or longer. The more members of the family who become monks and the longer they are monks, the greater the merit they earn for the deceased to go to heaven.

Services are usually held at the mortuary or funeral home. Family members, dressed in black or white, gather with friends and monks to pray for the soul of the deceased. The immediate family usually sits on the floor surrounding the open casket. The perfume of burning incense fills the air along with the sound of chanting monks.

A master of ceremonies will recount the life of the deceased and his accomplishments and this speech is repeated by members of the family. In this way, the family pays their respects to their loved one and pronounces the finality of the person's death. At one point the master of ceremonies will announce that the soul of the deceased should leave for the next life so that indeed, the spirit of the deceased will leave and go away.

The casket, with a rope attached, might be carried out of the chapel with family members and mourners following in procession. The group would proceed around the building, symbolizing the transition from one world to the next.

Cremation would follow the funeral service. In Laos, the oldest son used to light the funeral pyre; today in Hawai'i he symbolically performs this task by pushing the button at the crematory. Following cremation, the family will place the ashes and bones in an urn. Lucky is the family member who might find a piece of gold filling amongst the ashes.

Gifts of money in an envelope are customary. Refreshments and food are generally provided following the service which can last up to two hours. Families traditionally hold a funerary feast one hundred days after the funeral.

Upon returning home from a funeral, Lao people, like the Chinese, will wash their face with water perfumed with pomelo leaves, an act of purification.

Throughout the year in Hawai'i, there are innumerable events, holidays, festivals and celebrations originating within ethnic communities. Chambers of commerce, heritage groups, cultural organizations and churches sponsor concerts, art exhibits, dance recitals, craft and food festivals, beauty pageants, parades, street fairs, athletic events and other festivities designed to build awareness in and observe cultural traditions that have survived the generations.

The Japanese community's Cherry Blossom Festival, the Chinese community's Narcissus Festival and the Filipino community's Fiesta Filipina are a few of the annual ethnic celebrations, each culminating with the crowning of a beauty queen. Koreans observe the anniversary of the arrival of the first immigrants during January in significant years and the Portuguese commemorate their community's immigration in October.

Heroes are paid homage, too. King Kamehameha was once honored with great pageantry by the Hawaiian community; today the anniversary of his death is a statewide holiday featuring a parade and activities for residents and tourists alike. José Rizal, hero of Philippine independence is honored in December by many Filipino groups. Tongans honor their king's birthday with an annual celebration.

ANNUAL CULTURAL CELEBRATIONS AND FAMILY TRADITIONS

Scottish Heritage Week, Greek Festival, Samoan Flag Day, Okinawan Festival and other community wide events celebrate ethnic traditions through food, music, dance, art and the simple gathering of people. There always seems to be something "ethnic" going on in Hawai'i every week, especially on O'ahu.

Then there are the annual cultural celebrations that take place in a multitude of homes in Hawai'i, among families and within families. These are the traditions and customs handed down from one generation to the next that are not publicly celebrated but quietly observed by families who gather together for these special times. Along with the observance of family members' rites of passage, these cultural celebrations form the basis of family traditions in Hawai'i.

As midnight approaches on New Year's Eve, a cacophony of popping and cracking is heard in Honolulu, a thunderous roar of sound that crescendos at the stroke of midnight. Cascading showers of colorful stars light the skies and the whistle of rockets pierces the air above the deafening sound of long strings of firecrackers.

By 12:15 a.m. New Year's Day, it's over. Silence is intermittently broken with a few more pops and cracks. A cloud of smoke hovers over the city of Honolulu and the red remnants of firecrackers line the streets and sidewalks.

Welcoming the new year is one of those "only in Hawai'i" experiences – a festive and symbolic time incorporating many customs from many ethnic traditions. Fireworks, a Chinese custom, is just one of those traditions that say goodbye to the passing year and welcome to the future.

Tradition throughout the world expresses the hope that the New Year will be different and better than the passing year. After all, January was named for the Roman god Janus whose name comes from *janua*, the Latin word for door. Janus is always pictured with two faces, one looking backward and one looking forward.

Indulging in libations, food and fun to welcome the new year is a practice of people everywhere, dating back to ancient times when a New Year's feast was a time for bonding family relationships and alliances. People dine at restaurants or go to hotel ballrooms and nightclubs which feature special entertainment. Music, champagne, dancing, noisemakers, streamers, and strains of Auld Lang Syne put the old year to rest and welcome the new year. Other revelers might attend Honolulu's First Night events where artists, musicians, theatrical performers and dancers provide amusement to people of all ages in the downtown Honolulu area in a non-alcoholic environment.

In homes, families and friends gather to toast the new year and celebrate over an array of food and drink. Games of chance – poker, mah jong, *payute* (a card game), *sakura* (Japanese cards) – are played, ending the year with good fortune or foretelling the fortunes of the year ahead.

Fireworks at midnight has been a long standing tradition in Hawai'i practiced by all ethnic groups and all ages. Its purpose is to chase away evil spirits with noise and its practice has prevailed despite health and safety issues and restrictions on the type of fireworks permitted and the time they are allowed during the New Year holiday.

The arrival of the New Year is celebrated by everyone in Hawai'i in some way. For Asians in Hawai'i – Japanese, Okinawan, Korean, Chinese, Vietnamese, and Laotian – the New Year is the most significant cultural celebration of the year. For the Chinese and Vietnamese communities, the

Lunar New Year – the first day of the first month of the lunar year – is also observed, sometime between January 19 and February 20. For the Laotian community a time closest to April 13-15, the Buddhist New Year, is set aside for a celebration.

In Asia, the new year was recognized as the beginning of spring and the beginning of new life, based on the lunar calendar. In ancient times when farming was important to family life and survival, spring was the season for planting and the ensuing rains would nurture the crops for an abundant fall harvest. And, the New Year was a time for family reunions. Visiting with the extended family might occur only at this time of the year and much importance was placed on this activity.

Today, the arrival of spring and the planting of crops is secondary to the reunion of families and the ritual partaking of special foods that are painstakingly prepared to further carry on the traditions of the New Year celebrations of years past. Each ethnic group prepares its special foods that symbolically celebrate the passing of the old year and the optimism of the new year.

Traditional foods for Asian New Year celebrations in Hawai'i: Japanese kagami mochi *with tangerine, Chinese* gau *and Korean* duk.

But first, Asian tradition calls for a ritual house cleansing before the start of the new year, an important custom performed to remove any evil spirits or bad omens from the house that have gathered during the previous year. A third generation Japanese woman recalled the task of cleaning house before the new year: "We had to clean the house from top to bottom, wash all the windows, change the *tatami* (straw floor mats). We would get new toothbrushes, new towels and new clothes. And there wasn't any fighting and swearing, you just did it."

A Caucasian man, married to a second generation Korean woman, approaches the new year with little humor. "She makes me clean my closet and throw out old clothes. Then we have to clean the house – not my idea of a good time during the holidays. My wife's Korean, you know!"

Cleaning the house was viewed as an important part of the New Year ritual within the recent past in Hawai'i, but it is one of those traditions that is disappearing in contemporary island life. While some still observe this tradition today, many more, especially women, note that cleaning house for the new year is the one cultural tradition they have quickly abandoned!

Other folk wisdom among Asians prevailed during the new year celebration, some of which is observed today in Hawai'i. Rubbish would never be swept out the front door, only the back door, otherwise one would be sweeping away the good fortune of the family. Doors and windows would be opened on New Year's Eve, allowing the old year to get out of the house. Once New Year's Day arrives, there can't be any cleaning or sweeping because one would be cleaning out good spirits that have come to settle for the New Year.

The New Year further signals the closure of business transactions of the previous year, the repayment of all debts, and the end to feuds and disagreements. Wardrobes are refurbished, resolutions for the new year are made and offerings are made to the gods.

Tradition among Asians also dictates that nothing be cut on New Year's Day. Knives, scissors and other sharp objects are put away for fear that blood will be drawn on this day. And, more importantly, one would not want to cut the continuity of luck in the New Year. Thus, most families will prepare traditional foods before the arrival of New Year's Day.

The New Year, both calendar and lunar, was, at one time, the day for birthday celebrations. Everyone was a year older on New Year's Day or on the seventh day of the year according to Chinese tradition.

Visiting relatives and friends was a common practice during the New Year celebration period which can last for several days. Popular Asian lore holds that if the first visitor on New Year's Day is a male, good luck will prevail for the year.

Further, some will note that the actions of the first day of the year foretold the rest of the year. If you slept all day, you would sleep the rest of the year. If you cried, you would cry the rest of the year. If you loaned something on New Year's Day, you would be lending all year. If the first day was a pleasant and happy one, so would go the rest of the year. Arguments and disagreements were to be avoided on the first day of the year.

While popular lore may not be recognized by everyone in Hawai'i today, there are many who observe these folk ways and practices and assemble the colors, symbols and food that play an important role in this joyous season of family reunions. For Japanese, Okinawan, Korean, Chinese and Vietnamese families in Hawai'i the celebration of the calendar or lunar New Year is of great cultural significance and importance.

Shogatsu, The Japanese and Okinawan New Year Celebration

Considered the most important cultural celebration for Japanese people throughout the world *Shogatsu* (New Year) is viewed as the time to conclude the activities of the passing year and to begin activities with a fresh new outlook. In Hawai'i, the new year celebration is so important that given the choice of Christmas Eve or New Year's Eve off by employers, many Japanese and Okinawans will usually opt for New Year's Eve so that they can prepare for this important celebration. Of the many customs and practices associated with the New Year, the following are those most practiced by individuals and families of Japanese and Okinawan ancestry in Hawai'i.

On New Year's Eve, *soba* (buckwheat noodles) is eaten in Japan as a symbol of long life being transferred from the old year to the new year. This traditional noodle is called *toshikoshi soba* (year crossing soba). Many families in Hawai'i observe this custom today though some prefer a bowl of *saimin*, an Hawaiian soup and noodle dish, to greet the new year. Okinawan families might also include pig's feet soup on their menu for New Year's Eve. For them, pork is an important celebration food and in earlier times, the slaughtering of a pig just before New Year's Day would begin the traditional celebration activities.

At the stroke of midnight or early on the morning of January 1, many people go to Buddhist temples and Shinto shrines to pray and receive blessings for the new year. Temples and shrines are lit with lanterns, symbolizing hope for the new year. Buddhist temple bells toll 108 times, each

The kadomatsu *is a traditional New Year decoration for many island Japanese families.*

stroke of the gong representing the worldly passions of individuals which are to be overcome. Cleansing rituals are performed at Shinto shrines as the Bishop sprinkles water with a leafy branch.

White prayer papers attached to a long wand are waved to confer a New Year's blessing. Amulets or charms for good fortune and safety are distributed for a small donation. *Hatsu mode*, the first visit to the temple or shrine is an important ritual still practiced today in Hawai'i.

Japanese and Okinawan families in Hawai'i display the *kadomatsu* (gates of pine) a tradition that dates back to the Edo period of Japan. An arrangement of pine sprigs and three slant cut stalks of bamboo, bound together with cording representing Shinto sacred rope, the kadomatsu stands for morality, virtue and constancy. It may also include fern leaves for expanding good fortune throughout the years and plum sprigs suggesting purity and sweetness. Together the elements symbolize good wishes for a long, strong and prosperous life. Kadomatsu are displayed several days before January 1 and removed on January 7, ceremonially burned for purification or tossed away in flowing water.

Foods take on special meanings for the New Year. Most significant is *mochi*, the rice cake made from steamed and pounded glutinous rice. Mochi symbolizes long life and its homonym is *kane*, the word for wealth.

Days before January 1, many families engage in *mochi tsuki* (the rice pounding ceremony). Glutinous rice is soaked in water overnight, and steamed the next morning. Morsels of steamed rice might be given to young children before it is placed in an *usu* (a wood or stone mortar) and pounded with a *kine* (a long handled mallet). When the rice is smooth and sticky, it is shaped, usually by the women and children, into small cakes and filled with *an* (sweet bean paste).

This ritual of mochi pounding is performed by a few Japanese and Okinawan families in Hawai'i today who might gather many generations together. Most families purchase their mochi at specialty stores and supermarkets which provide a convenient supply throughout the year.

Kagami-mochi, literally mirror mochi, is a display of two large mochi cakes stacked one on top of the other and topped off with a tangerine. The two rounded cakes symbolize the sun and the moon;

Using a traditional usu *(mortar) and* kine *(pestle), Thomas Tomotani pounds steamed glutinous rice for mochi a few days prior to New Year's Day. Once pounded, the warm mass of rice is quickly shaped into flat discs and filled with sweetened bean paste.*

two for increased good fortune, rounded to represent smoothness and harmony. The mochi represents mirrors into which Amaterasu, the Sun Goddess, looked when she emerged from her cave.

The tangerine has replaced the *dai dai* (bigarde or bitter lemons) once used to symbolize new life from the seeds. The pronunciation of dai dai is identical to an expression meaning generation after generation, thus it is symbolic of long life and good health. This fruit matures in winter and if left on the tree becomes green again, signifying rebirth. Since this fruit is not cultivated today, tangerines are used which, like the dai dai, has many seeds representing many offspring.

The kagami mochi rests upon *gohei* (white paper) representing cloth offerings to the gods. In Hawai'i, the paper might display one of seven gods of good fortune. Ebisu, a fishing god is one of the most popular figures. A piece of seaweed or cuttlefish might accompany the tangerine at the top. Originally a crayfish or lobster would be displayed, symbolizing old age because of its bent body, but wishes for a youthful spirit and longevity.

The kagami-mochi assembly is displayed in a place of honor in the home or in the *tokonoma*, the alcove usually reserved for a floral arrangement found in many island Japanese homes. The mochi is broken into pieces on January 3 and eaten and the whole display dismantled on January 11. Kagami-mochi is never cut with a knife for to do so would be to cut up the good fortune it represents.

On New Year's Day morning, many families gather to eat *ozoni*, a soup prepared with mochi and vegetables. While recipes and ingredients vary from family to family, the mochi is always a key ingredient. Eating ozoni is supposed to give one strength and assure prosperity for the new year.

Sake is served each member of the family with the male head of the household taking the first sip. If one were drinking tea on New Year's morning, *umeboshi* (pickled plum) would be added to the tea for good health.

Feasting on a variety of foods continues on New Year's Day. *Sashimi* (sliced raw fish) is traditional in Hawai'i and it is usually a red fish like *ahi* (yellow fin tuna) or *aku* (skipjack tuna) replacing the *tai* (red sea bream) favored in Japan. The demand for ahi and aku during the days before January 1 drives the price of these fish sky high.

In addition to ozoni and sashimi, Japanese and Okinawan families in Hawai'i will usually include one or more of the following items in their menu for the new year celebration:

Kazunoko (herring eggs) eaten for fertility and wishes for a family blessed with many children.

Kuromame (sweetened black beans) eaten for good health and future success.

Kobumaki (seaweed wrapped around fish) tied with *kampyo* (gourd), eaten for happiness. Carrots, pork and *gobo* (burdock root) may also be included.

Kinton (mashed sweet potato and nuts) eaten for good fortune. Whole chestnuts are included, symbolizing gold or money or prosperity.

Kamaboko (fish cake) eaten because of the lucky combination of colors, red and white, that will bring happiness.

Renkon (lotus root), sliced crosswise, is symbolic of the wheel of life and a sacred plant in Buddhist tradition.

Nantu, a steamed rice cake wrapped in banana leaves, is traditonal among Okinawan families.

Since the New Year celebration is a family time, for many it is also a time to visit grave sites. Those visiting grave sites offer mochi to the spirits, along with rice, sake, salt, and water. *Konbu* (seaweed) is also offered as a symbol of long life.

New year celebrations last for several days. Recently, *Bonen Kai* and *Shinen Kai* (pre and post New Year's parties) have been held by many Japanese businesses in Hawaii. Bonen Kai means forgetting the cares and a party is held to forget the feuds, and stress of the passing year. Shinen Kai is a welcome the new year celebration and considered good luck for businessmen.

Visiting friends and relatives is part of the activity and festivity of Shogatsu. For the Japanese community in Hawai'i, this celebration emphasizes its rich cultural heritage by bringing together its most significant aspect: the family.

The Korean New Year Celebration

"No matter where we were on New Year's Eve, we had to be home by midnight," recalled a Korean woman referring to the arrival of the New Year, the most significant celebration for Korean families in Hawai'i. Like their Asian counterparts, the ritual of house cleaning, the completion of business deals and the eating of traditional foods are still observed by island Korean families.

A Korean couple recalled the family custom of displaying a piece of *yut* (sticky candy) on New Year's Eve. It was left out overnight in a noticeable spot for the spirits that return to earth at this auspicious time. The spirits would hopefully find the candy and eat it. The stickiness of the candy, however, would not allow the spirits to talk – therefore they wouldn't be able to say bad things about the household to the heavenly gods.

One of the original Korean immigrants to Hawai'i remembered being told as a child not to go to sleep on New Year's Eve. "If we did, our eyebrows would turn white. So if by chance someone in the family went to sleep, we would paint their eyebrows white!"

The same woman recalled that on New Year's Day, everyone wore new clothes to greet the New Year. Children and young people would pay their respects to their parents and elders, visiting the homes of relatives and friends. In return they were given coins wrapped in rice paper.

Why Koreans Eat Yak Bap

Yak bap is a steamed rice confection enjoyed by Koreans during the New Year celebration and at all festive occasions commemorating life's passages. Made of glutinous rice steamed with dried red dates, chestnuts, pine nuts and honey, it is often referred to as a medicinal rice.

Yak bap originated over a thousand years ago during the reign of King Sochi, the twenty-first King of the Silla Dynasty. Legend says the king received a letter carried by a crow while he was having a picnic in his garden. The inscription of the letter read: "If opened, two shall die; if not opened, one shall die."

The king's advisors explained the message: "One" is the King, and "two" are other people. The King opened the letter and the message read "Shoot into the harp case." The King went back to his palace and shot an arrow into the harp case. As crimson blood oozed out of the harp case, the king looked in and saw his Queen and a monk embracing, floating in their own blood.

The Queen had been in love with the monk for some time and had planned to murder the King that night. Thanks to the crow, the King escaped. The King declared Crow Thanksgiving Day on the fifteenth day of the First Moon to repay the kindness of the crow who saved his life. It has come to be celebrated on January 15 with the preparation and serving of yak bap in honor of the crow.

While some of these practices have not continued today, one tradition that has is the eating of *duk kuk*. Duk is a rice cake similar to Japanese mochi, kuk is the soup in which it is served. *Hind duk* (a log shaped rice cake) is a symbol of longevity, and is traditionally eaten for good luck during the New Year celebration.

Duk is prepared from steamed glutinous rice, pounded to a smooth paste and shaped into logs about an inch in diameter. The logs are cut into coin sized pieces and served in chicken or beef broth, topped with shreds of marinated and braised beef, eggs, green onions and crumbled seaweed.

The New Year's feast might also include *kalbi jim* (braised short ribs), *pin dae duk* (a pancake of ground mung beans), and *nrum juk* (skewered seasoned beef and vegetables fried in an egg batter). *Mun doo* (a dumpling of pork, tofu and vegetables) is often served by local Korean families with the duk kuk. *Kim chi*, the spicy pickled cabbage of Korean cuisine, would, of course be served.

Yak bap or *yak sik*, a steamed rice confection, is another traditional food served on New Year's Day in Hawai'i. Sticky rice is steamed with chestnuts, dates and pine nuts, sweetened with honey and darkened with soy sauce. Some families prepare their own yak bap while others purchase it at Korean grocery stores.

New Year's Day is a day for feasting and family reunion for Koreans in Hawai'i. For some of the more recent immigrant families, the celebration and visiting might continue up until January 15 when the first full moon of the year is welcomed.

According to ancient tradition, it was believed that the first to see the moon would have a lucky year. The moon foretold feast or famine, rain or drought, good times or bad times. On the night before the first full moon, a special doll made of straw containing coins was thrown out in a public place. The *cheyong* (doll) symbolized invading devils and were thrown out to protect the household.

While these folk beliefs are not as prevalent today, some families continue to commemorate this first full moon of the year. Dishes of five grains and five vegetables are prepared and eaten for this special day which culminates the family observance of the New Year.

The Chinese Lunar Celebration

Kung Hee Fat Choy! (a prosperous new year) is the popular greeting in Hawai'i as the Chinese community celebrates the lunar new year with much fanfare and festivity. Sometime between January 19 and February 20, the first day of the first month of the lunar year is celebrated with family reunions, feasting and honoring of ancestors.

Preparations for the New Year begin up to a month before. Honolulu's Chinatown is abuzz with activity: shopkeepers sell special foods to be prepared for the celebration and weekend street festivals feature favorite Chinese foods and sweets.

The Chinese lion parades down the streets, stopping to wish shopkeepers luck for the new year. The elaborate and colorful Chinese lion symbolizes life, luck and virility. Young members of Chinese societies don the lion's headdress and dance to

Why We Celebrate the New Year

A legend of China recounts how people along the Yellow River Basin lived a simple, nomadic life, very content and happy. On a cold winter evening a mysterious being attacked the village and destroyed the villagers' property.

A village meeting was held and precautions taken to protect them from the intruder. Nothing happened and people went about their daily routines. Then the mysterious being struck again, causing even greater damage to lives and property.

Again, the villagers gathered and prepared for their safety. And again, nothing happened and people went about their normal activity, feeling secure and safe. But the mysterious force struck a third time, causing much loss and great fear among the villagers.

An elderly scholar had studied the intrusions, watching the stars and heavenly bodies and recording their movements. He explained that the intruder came when the heavenly bod-ies were in a particular order and after the sun had appeared 365 times.

The villagers studied this theory closely and learned that the intruder feared three things: the color red, illumination and noise. They called the intruder Nien or year.

On the following 365th day, preparations were made for the return of Nien. Houses were lit with lanterns, objects were painted bright red and loud noises were made until dawn of the next day.

The villagers' plan worked and the mysterious intruder did not reappear. It was decided that from then on, a thanksgiving ceremony would be held every 365th evening to thank all the gods for their blessings. And that the same preparations would be made for the return of Nien, scaring away the evil deeds of the spirits. Thus we celebrate the new year, chasing away evil with fireworks and celebrating with festivity and food.

the rhythm of drums and gongs, stopping at shops and receiving money from shopkeepers. A roar of firecrackers accompanies the lion dance, further warding off evil spirits for the new year.

Food, is especially important for Chinese New Year. Of particular importance is *nien-gao* or *gao*, a steamed, cylindrical shaped, sticky pudding made of sweet rice flour and brown sugar, usually wrapped in a ti leaf. Nien gao means year cake and is also a homonym for the words year high. To the Chinese it has great meaning: hoping that the coming year will be filled with the realization of high hopes and aspirations.

Nien-gao is very symbolic for Hawai'i's Chinese families. The stickiness of the glutinous rice flour signifies that the family will be very cohesive and stick together. The round shape symbolizes the reunion of the family and the sugar stands for the sweetness of life. Sesame seeds sprinkled on top represent a desire for many children and the red date topping of the cake is for good luck.

Nien-gao can be seen in abundance in Chinese sweet shops during the days preceding the Chinese New Year. Of course, many families make their own gao, according to treasured family recipes. On the second day of the New Year, families open the cake and cut it into pieces, sharing it with relatives and friends.

Tin nien, New Year's Eve, is a time for thanksgiving for all the year's blessings. Families gather to feast on a sumptuous meal in honor of the occasion. Foods resembling auspicious things are served: spring rolls resembling bricks of gold, clams indicating a receptivity to good fortune or a whole fish symbolizing bounty.

On New Year's Day, no animal's life is to be taken, therefore a vegetarian dish called *jai* is eaten all day. Families gather early on New Year's Day, before going to school and work, to partake of this traditional New Year's dish, also known as Monk's food. Many ingredients can be included in jai, varying from family to family:

Long rice is for longevity.

Foo jook (dried bean curd) is for blessings to the house.

Mushrooms welcome spring.

Fat choy (a black, kinky hair like algae) is symbolic of wealth.

Wun ngee, mook ngee or *chin ngee* is a fungus that usually grows on oak trees. It is exceptionally durable when dry and has come to mean longevity and immortality.

Peas and water chestnuts whose roundness symbolize unity.

Bak ko (gingko nuts) represent silver ingots.

Gum choy (dried golden lilies) are symbolic of wealth.

Hua sung (peanuts) are symbolic of birth and promotion.

How see (oysters) represent good undertakings, good tidings, good affairs and good business. In keeping with the rule of not taking life on New Year's Day, dried oysters are used.

Sweet meats or candied fruits and vegetables are also a must for Chinese New Year. Hexagonal shaped candy boxes with removable fan shaped compartments display a variety of fruits and vegetables that convey a symbolic wish for the new year.

Another prized delicacy of the Chinese New Year Celebration is *toong mai* (puffed glutinous rice cakes). These crunchy squares contain toasted rice, roasted peanuts, finely grated ginger, and toasted sesame seeds held together by a coating of candied syrup. Originally made by the Hakka descendants, these delicacies can be found throughout the year along with sweet meats and other delicacies in Honolulu's Chinatown sweet shops.

On New Year's Day, many Chinese children continue an age old tradition of paying their respects to their elders by visiting them and pouring tea for them. In return the children receive lisee, given as an expression of good wishes and gratitude by parents, relatives and friends to unmarried children only.

Chinatown shops supply posters and decorative items especially for the lunar new year celebration. These bright red calligraphic posters add gaiety to the celebration while exclaiming wishful hopes for the new year. They decorate the house and enliven everyone's spirits. Couplets written on long narrow strips of paper are also placed at the doorway of businesses.

Sui sin fah (the narcissus flower) is also a part of the New Year tradition in Hawai'i. Timing the bloom of the Flower of the Water Fairy is especially important since the closer to New Year's Day that the blossoms open, the more good fortune they will bring.

Visiting relatives and friends is an important activity during the Chinese New Year celebration and no one visits empty handed. Oranges or tangerines are taken as a symbol of good luck for the recipient, and one always returns home with a few given back in return.

The Chinese New Year celebration comes to a close on the fifteenth day of the lunar year, the

A traditional sweetmeats box might be filled for the lunar new year celebration by Chinese and Vietnamese families. Each item has a symbolic wish for the new year: lotus root (clockwise from top) for endless friendship; squash for the long continuous line of descendants; carrots represent wealth; coconut for a warm relationship between father and son; ginger for good health; melon seeds are a wish for many children; and lotus seeds (center) are for the continuous production of sons.

day of the first full moon. Another delicacy is prepared: *yuan hsiao*, glutinous rice cakes, shaped into balls, served in a sweetened soup. In days past, a Lantern Festival was held on this day and people decorated their homes with colorful lanterns. This event is occasionally staged in Honolulu by Chinese organizations and societies.

Tet, The Vietnamese Lunar Celebration

Like the Chinese, the Vietnamese community in Hawai'i celebrates *Tet* (the lunar new year) with much festivity and activity, drawing upon the customs of their homeland. It is the most important holiday for Vietnamese, a combination of Christmas and New Year celebrations rolled into one.

Tet is a time for family reunion, gift exchanging, feasting and merrymaking. *Giao thua*, the transition moment or midnight on New Year's Eve, is a time for fireworks and temple visits. Prayers are offered to ancestral spirits and everyone looks forward to the new year with optimism.

Vietnamese celebrate Tet with similar foods and rituals as the Chinese. Red is the favorite color for this holiday, symbolizing good luck and happiness. Houses are cleaned and decorated with New Year wishes on red paper. Children pay their respects to their elders, receiving lisee in return. The pink peach blossom and the yellow apricot blossom are symbolic of the arrival of spring and are used to decorate doorways of houses during Tet.

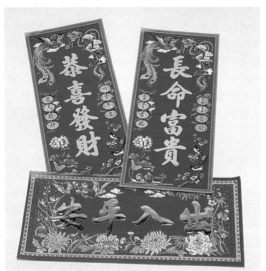

Couplets express good wishes, prosperity and health for the new year and are displayed by Vietnamese and Chinese families during the lunar new year celebration.

Bang chung or *banh tet* is the typical Tet food, a glutinous rice cake filled with meat and beans, wrapped in a banana leaf and steamed for several hours. Sweetmeats, jai, and oranges are all important to the Tet celebration among Vietnamese as they are for the Chinese community.

Pee Mai, The Laotian New Year Festival

Celebrated on or near April 13-15, *Pee Mai* (the Laotian New Year festival) brings together Hawai'i's small but cohesive Laotian community. Regarded as more important than the lunar new year, Pee Mai centers around Buddhist traditions and the Lao Buddhist Society Temple. Because the Lao temple in Honolulu is small and cannot accommodate the community, many festivities for Pee Mai are held in public parks and school auditoriums. Festivities may be held over two weekends to accommodate the working community.

The celebration begins with the ritual of cleaning common to all Asian new year celebrations. In homes, statues of Buddha are cleansed with perfumed flower water, symbolizing the bathing of Buddha by sweet rain. At the Lao Buddhist Society Temple, the statue of Buddha is brought down from its perch and everyone participates in this ritual cleansing.

Then in a park setting, the fun begins as people splash water on each other, symbolically cleansing each other for the new year. Socializing and traditional foods conclude the first day of the community wide celebration.

Visits to the temple are important to the Pee Mai observance. Each person brings along some sand, each grain representing one bad thing you've done in the year past. Bringing the sand ceremonially removes these bad things so one may start the new year with a clean slate.

On another day, the community gathers, clad in traditional Laotian costume to conclude the new year celebration. A variety of traditional foods are prepared and offered to the monks who preside over this ritual filled day. Socializing, music and ritual are prominent on this day.

A tower of flowers proclaims that *su kwon* or *baci*, the health ceremony, is to be conducted. This ritual tying of string around the wrist calls back the wandering *kwan* (soul spirits) insuring good health and happiness for the new year.

Another important ritual is the pouring of water by worshipers from one vessel into another, symbolically pouring away one's cares and worries. While the individual prays, the monks chant to help the process.

Children anxiously await the moment for the releasing of birds, purchased and carried in little boxes. In a symbolic ritual that helps to free the individual of cares and worries, dozens of birds are set free.

The last ritual of the new year celebration gathers together parents and elders. Young people petition their elders for forgiveness for any wrongs of the previous year and for blessings in the coming year.

Besides the community wide events, family and friends gather over the three days to feast upon their traditional foods and to socialize. *Laap* is the most important food for Lao celebrations and it would certainly be served at this one.

Rich in cultural and religious traditions, Pee Mai gathers the Lao community on O'ahu together once a year to participate in the rituals that have engaged families for generations.

Like the rest of the United States, people in Hawai'i celebrate Easter as a religious observance or as the beginning of spring and a time for renewal. Special family dinners observe the day and according to American tradition, ham or spring lamb are featured. The dying of Easter eggs, Easter egg hunts, Easter baskets and bonnets are all part of festivities in the islands.

Some Portuguese families in Hawai'i continue two traditions related to the Easter season that are unique: Malassada Day, observed on Shrove Tuesday, and the Holy Ghost Festival observed on Pentecost Sunday, seven weeks after Easter Sunday.

Malassada Day

Malassadas are fried doughnuts rolled in sugar that are a specialty of the Portuguese kitchen. They were not allowed during the Christian Lenten season since they were

Loretta Hess of Nova Esperança, one of many Portuguese heritage groups in Hawai'i, cooks up a batch of malassadas on Malassada Day to be enjoyed by people of all ethnic backgrounds.

originally fried in lard, a meat product that was forbidden during this period. So on the Tuesday before the period of abstinence from meat and meat products began, people used up their lard and made malassadas.

A number of Portuguese families in Hawai'i celebrate Malassada Day on the Tuesday before Ash Wednesday, the first day of Lent. This day is also known as Dia de Entrudo, Mardi Gras, Shrove Tuesday or Fat Tuesday.

Popular lore explains that malassadas originated because a housewife had a batch of what appeared to be bad dough which didn't rise. Not wanting to waste the dough, she pinched off a piece and threw it in a pan of hot fat. The word malassada comes from the verb *assar* meaning to bake or roast; the prefix *mal* means bad. Together it means bad dough for baking.

The tradition of making malassadas on Shrove Tuesday was observed in the Azores and Madeira, the original home of Hawai'i's Portuguese community. The tradition continues in many home kitchens today or at Malassada Day celebrations at community centers. Lard has generally been replaced by vegetable oils today and family recipes vary widely. Malassadas are often found at carnivals, state fairs and other community events throughout the year on all islands.

Flower bedecked statues of the Holy family await the Holy Ghost Festival procession at the Punchbowl Holy Ghost Church on O'ahu.

Another tradition of some island Portuguese kitchens that continues is the making of *massa savada* (traditional sweet bread). Started with grated potato and yeast, massa savada is shaped into rounds and baked with an egg in the center, symbolizing fertility and new life. Like its cousin *pao duce* (sweet bread), massa savada used to be baked in *fornos* (igloo shaped stone ovens) that once dotted Portuguese communities throughout the islands.

The Holy Ghost Festival

For Portuguese families of the Catholic faith, The Holy Ghost Festival is an important community tradition celebrated on Pentecost Sunday, the fiftieth day after Easter. This festival was brought to Hawai'i by the Portuguese families who came to work on the sugar plantations.

The Holy Ghost Festival, is a reenactment of thanksgiving by Queen Isabel to the Holy Spirit for saving her people from death by starvation. The Festival originated in the town of Alenquer on mainland Portugal in the thirteenth century. Queen Isabel, who had great faith in the Holy Ghost, promised to give away her earthly possessions to save her starving people.

One story says that a miracle occurred and the drought that was causing the famine went away. Another story says that a ship laden with cattle and wheat veered off course and arrived in Lisbon. Queen Isabel purchased the food and fed her starving people. Still another story says that Queen

Isabel was instructed to build a church in honor of the Holy Ghost. The church was built in Alenquer and its consecration was an occasion for sharing meat and bread with the poor people of the area. It was her wish that this tradition continue every year at Pentecost and thus the Confraternity of the Holy Ghost was founded and preserved the tradition of feeding poor people.

In Hawai'i the Holy Ghost Festival is a three day celebration observed at a few Catholic churches, culminating a seven week observance following Easter Sunday. Seven feasts, known as *domingas*, begin on the first Saturday after Easter, each honoring a different figure in the Catholic religion or Portuguese history and each sponsored by a family.

The highlight of the Holy Ghost season is a three day festival that begins on the Friday night of the seventh week. This event was originally a feast for the poor and hungry where donated meat and bread were distributed by the church priest, symbolically recreating Queen Isabel's charity to her people. Some churches follow this tradition today and provide meat, bread, stew, a bowl of soup or *laulaus* (steamed taro leaves and pork) to those attending the festival.

Churches become fair grounds where food booths, games and socializing are the activities of the second day. Traditional foods like *tremoco* (lupine beans) are prepared and games like *bisca*, a Portuguese card game, may be played. A band or choral concert, folk dancing, and festivity continue into the evening.

The Holy Ghost Festival culminates on Sunday with the coronation of the Holy Ghost queen. A procession of banners, floral floats and the queen's crown may be part of the festivities of some churches. Mass is held in honor of the day and at the conclusion, the priest crowns the Holy Ghost queen.

Activities of the Holy Ghost Festival are as varied as the churches and congregations that host them. Its traditions span many generations in Hawai'i and is observed by many families, particularly on O'ahu and Maui.

Hinamatsuri: **Girls' Day**

A special day just for little girls, *Hinamatsuri* (Girls' Day) is celebrated by Japanese and Okinawan families in Hawai'i with a special meal, rice cakes and dolls. Celebrated on March 3, the observance actually begins up to two weeks earlier when little girls unpack doll collections that were started at birth. This activity, repeated each year, is meant to teach discipline, patience, neatness and responsibility to the young girl. Sisters often share collections and the dolls are passed on from generation to generation.

The dolls depict an emperor with his empress and their court, dressed in brocaded garments, typical of the Japanese Heian Court (794-1185 A.D.). The tiered display is often quite elaborate though having just an emperor and empress doll are equally important to the celebration. According to local folk wisdom, the display must be taken down on March 3 if you want your daughter to marry.

Dolls are displayed for Girls' Day, March 3. Emperor and empress dolls are positioned at the top of the red tiered display, with ladies in waiting, musicians, retainers and guards below. Lanterns, ceremonial trays, tea sets, chests for clothing, make-up stands, palanquins, serving boxes and trees complete the formal display.

Girls' Day is not without its special food: *hishi mochi*. This diamond shaped rice cake is made in three colors: white representing the snow of winter or purity; red (actually pink) for the flowers of spring or energy; and green for the freshness of summer or fertility. There is no color for autumn since it is hoped there will be no autumn in little girls' lives.

Hishi mochi is made in the shape of a medicinal leaf thought to have the property of giving long life to the eater. Other special foods for Girls' Day include *sekihan* (dish of rice cooked with red beans), *ochagashi* (tea cake), *umani* (dish of cooked vegetables with meat) and *shirozake* (white rice wine).

Paper peach blossoms, a symbol of peace, are given to little girls on this day to convey the wish that she will be gentle and tranquil and have a peaceful married life. Family dinners at home or at a restaurant cap off this special day for young girls.

Tango-no-sekku: Boys' Day

Colorful carp playfully "swim" in the trade winds above many houses in Hawai'i on May 5, commemorating *Tango-no-sekku* (Boys' Day). A tradition that can be witnessed on all islands, it is a special day for boys that also includes family dinners, dolls and special foods.

Koi nobori (carp streamers) made of paper or cloth are hung outside of homes on May 5, one for each boy in the house. Bamboo poles or flagpoles display the gaily colored carp. The size of the carp indicates ages: larger carp for the oldest child, smaller for the youngest. In recent years, the number of carp being flown represents the number of children in the household, boys and girls together.

The *koi* (carp) symbolizes masculinity. It is a spirited and hardy fish, believed to be able to swim upstream against a strong current and even surmount waterfalls. Legend says that a carp once

Koi *(carp) streamers "swim" atop roofs celebrating Boys' Day, May 5. In Hawai'i, each carp represents a child in the household, boys and girls together.*

swam all the way to heaven and became a dragon. It is also believed that carp have a long life. Thus the qualities of strength, perseverance and longevity have earned the carp a central role in the celebration of Boys' Day.

Dolls are also important for the celebration of Boys' Day. In ancient times, replicas of warriors and swordsmen were used like scarecrows to drive away insects and pests when they began to appear on crops in the fifth month of the year. Later these dolls were displayed indoors, teaching young boys manliness and to protect them from evil.

Male dolls depicting warriors, knights, courtiers and martial arts figures as well as their helmets, armor, and swords are arranged in tiers. Figures such as Momotaro, the peach boy, Benkei, the warrior priest, or other heroic warriors are also displayed.

Kashiwa mochi and *chimaki mochi* are made

especially for Boys' Day. Kashiwa mochi is a bean filled rice cake wrapped in an oak leaf. The oak is a sturdy and upright tree, considered positive attributes for a young boy. Chimaki mochi is wrapped in bamboo leaves. Chimaki is a play on words that could mean "a spirit bundled up tight."

White Sunday

A tradition of *Fa'a Samoa* (old Samoa) that has continued in Hawai'i is that of White Sunday, a special day in October that honors children in a Samoan family. Little kings and queens for a day, Samoan children are dressed up in brand new white clothes for the occasion. They take center stage at church services and are showered with attention on this day.

Particularly significant is that children are served first during the meals of the day. In traditional Samoan homes, adults eat first and children eat last. On White Sunday, children are honored and served first by their parents.

Reverend Daiya Amano of the Izumo Taishakyo Mission pours sake (rice wine) for Laura Koike as her mother Sumiko Koike lends a hand during a traditional Shichi-go-san ceremony on November 15.

Shichi-go-san: Seven-Five-Three

A childhood rite of passage called Shichi-go-san is sometimes observed by Japanese families in Hawai'i on November 15. A tradition dating back 400 years in Japan, boys and girls are dressed up in kimonos and taken to Shinto shrines for a special ceremony thanking the *kami* (spirits) for the child's protection and petitioning the kami for future blessings.

Shichi-go-san means seven-five-three and refers to the age of seven for girls, five for boys and three for both boys and girls. According to tradition, different articles of Japanese clothing were put on to symbolize a child's growth. Today it is a day for youngsters to be dressed up in kimonos, taken to the shrine and have their pictures taken. While few families on Oahu continue this tradition, neighbor island communities observe this day as well as Japanese families from Japan residing in Hawai'i today.

Memorial Day, was once an observance for soldiers who had died in defense of their country. It is now a day of remembering all loved ones who have died. Cemeteries in Hawaii abound with flowers on May 30 where families are known for keeping grave sites well tended and decorated throughout the year.

In addition to Memorial Day and special holidays throughout the year, almost every ethnic group in the islands pays tribute to their loved ones upon the first anniversary of death. Catholic Filipinos observe the one year anniversary of death with the saying of mass, a family gathering and socializing. All Souls Day on November 2 is another day Catholic Filipino families might visit gravesites, light candles and offer prayers for family members.

Buddhists of all ethnic backgrounds would observe the one year anniversary of death, followed by third, fifth, seventh, thirteenth, seventeenth, twenty-fifth, thirty-third, thirty-seventh and fiftieth year commemorations.

Each year, Chinese and Japanese families in Hawai'i observe special periods to remember deceased family members. These memorial periods are more than just decorating grave sites with flowers; it is a time to appease spirits with offerings and rituals that will insure the continued good fortune of the family on earth.

Ch'ing Ming:
Festival of Pure Brightness

Drive past a cemetery in April and you will see a colorful sight: flowers decorating grave sites, incense and candles burning, plates of food and fruit laid out and people gathering around. The sound of fireworks might be heard. It's not Memorial Day but its Chinese equivalent, Ch'ing Ming.

Ch'ing Ming or The Festival of Pure Brightness is a time for Chinese families to honor their deceased ancestors who, it is believed, are still exerting their influence over the living. In an expression of filial piety, some families pay homage each year to their ancestors.

Celebrated on the third day of the third moon or 106 days after the Winter Solstice, Ch'ing Ming is observed for thirty days when it is believed that the Heavenly Gates are open and the spirits of the deceased return to earth. Since they would be around the grave site, families visit the grave site and present offerings to win their favor.

In Hawai'i April 5 has been designated as the first day of Ch'ing Ming except in a leap year when April 4 is designated. The thirty day observance brings together families in a ritual that was embedded in the early Chinese immigrants and that has survived the passage of many generations.

The oldest son of a family carries the responsibility for observing Ch'ing Ming. But as one

Chinese woman related, it is really the wives of sons that carry on the tradition. The wives prepare the food, buy the candles, incense and paper money and call everyone to set the time and day of the family's observance.

During Ch'ing Ming, graves are swept, cleaned up and tidied by family members who coordinate their schedules and converge upon the site on a particular day. Offerings of food are brought to the cemetery. Two to three rib sections of a roasted pig is one of the traditional offerings, symbolically representing earth. A whole roast pig might be brought to the cemetery when the family feels especially blessed with good health, happiness and prosperity.

Fish, representing the sea and a whole chicken with head and feet representing heaven are also brought to the small altar. Items are whole, representing whole things of the earth. Tofu for blessings, oysters, shrimp, duck eggs, rice, sweet steamed buns, oranges, liquor and tea are also brought to the cemetery. Chopsticks are provided for everyone present.

A box of sand holds burning incense and red prayer candles. Members of the family in turn light *bau*, rectangular paper flat boats folded to hold paper gold and silver bullion. This offering of "money" is accompanied by three bows and a prayer for blessings and protection from ancestral spirits. More gold and silver paper money might be burned in large cans. The more money burned, the better for ancestral spirits to buy merits and services in the spiritual world.

A piece of the pork is left on the grave along with sugar buns, oranges and flowers for the spirits. The Earth God or caretaker is given a special offering of pork, salt egg, liquor, tea, a special pair of chopsticks and incense sticks. These are left to the side of the grave which is marked by *sarn bark*, a brilliant red and gold emblem signifying that the family has been there for their formal visit. An older member of the family chants a quotation to end the visit and firecrackers are burned to drive away the evil spirits.

Except for the few items of food left at the grave site, the rest of the food is eaten by the families either at the grave site, picnic style, or

Paraphernalia for the observance of Ch'ing Ming: stick incense or joss sticks resting atop yellow paper money; red prayer candles atop "hell" bank notes; red printed bau filled with gold and silver paper "bullion" to be burned by family members.

taken home for a family feast. The festivities may begin at sunrise but must end by sundown to avoid evil spirits at night.

Since spirits are active and traveling about during this period, many people in Hawai'i are cautious in their daily actions. Some do not go into the ocean to avoid any bad occurrences. One surfer laments that he cannot enjoy his sport during this month, respecting his family's wishes and not wanting to be the object of evil spirits.

One family reported that they had ignored the annual ritual of Ch'ing Ming for a deceased parent on the Mainland for several years. They experienced a series of bad events over an equal number of years. Finally, at his wife's urging, the husband went to the East Coast of the U.S. to perform the ritual at his parent's grave, outfitted with the proper food, and a coffee can and matches to light the paper money, incense, candles and firecrackers. The family's fate improved, which they owe to the observance of this ritual.

Ch'ing Ming is not only a memorial for ancestors but perhaps more importantly, another tradition which brings together families within the Chinese community. Parents deem this to be an important tradition and carefully teach their children the rituals, perhaps because they, too, want to be honored when they have departed.

Obon: Feast of the Dead

Ever since Buddhism was introduced to Japan, the memorial festival of *obon* has been celebrated to perpetuate the concept of filial piety through ancestor worship. Also known as *bon*, *urabon* or *bon-odori*, this Buddhist tradition has survived the waves of immigration to Hawai'i and is still observed by members of the Japanese and Okinawan communities on all islands.

Celebrated annually, obon is based on a legend from India. A disciple of Buddha saw that his deceased mother had been reborn among the Hungry Ghosts of Hell. She had once eaten meat but denied it so she was condemned to hanging upside down as punishment. Hungry as she was, she could not eat because food and water would turn to fire. Seeing this, the disciple earned merits and rescued his mother from hell and brought her to the shores of Nirvana. There she danced for joy and reveled in the abundance of food.

In Hawai'i, obon festivities at various Buddhist temples are scheduled in July and August. Families might begin the festivities by visiting grave sites, sweeping and cleaning them. *Manju* (a pastry filled with sweet bean paste), *mochi* (steamed rice cakes), simple foods and tea are offered to invite ancestral spirits back to earth.

Pine torches might be attached to bamboo and placed on gates to welcome spirits to the family home and a tub of water is made available for the spirits to wash their hands and feet. Lanterns are hung in front of houses to welcome spirits to their home. Incense is burned and offerings of food are made at the family altar in the home.

A memorial service at the temple will be attended by the family. Wooden tablets bearing the name of ancestors and deceased relatives are sometimes seen at temples. Offerings of food and incense are made on the wooden platforms; sutras are chanted and prayers offered.

On the final day of a family's observance, the spirits are said to return to the nether world and candle-lit lanterns are set adrift in a body of water to guide them back. Food and other sacred articles are placed in straw boats and set afloat to the Paradise of the Western Regions. The Floating Lanterns Festival can be observed at various sites throughout the State during obon season.

Bon dancing, a religious folk dance, occurs on the last night of the celebration, too. The dance of rejoicing for the souls, bon-odori is a colorful and festive affair. The *yagura* (musician's tower) stands in the center of a temple's open area, bright colored lanterns are strung around the perimeter of the grounds and food booths serving teriyaki sticks, saimin, shaved ice, mochi and other delicacies are in evidence. Dancers perform their stylized movements to the sound of recorded or live music that has a slow but rhythmic tempo. Small hand drums are used by Okinawan dancers.

Lanterns, dancing, music and a festival atmosphere characterize the Obon season in Hawai'i observed at Buddhist temples in July and August each year.

Once an open participatory event, bon dancing in Hawai'i has developed into an organized affair that varies from temple to temple and requires practice among the dancers for many months prior to the season. Bon odori also requires participants to be properly attired in a *happi coat* (short kimono like garment) or *yukata* (cotton kimono). Each dancer carries a *tenugui* (small hand towel) manipulated during the dance routine.

In Honolulu many participants are uniformly attired and organized like a club perpetuating the tradition of live music and the performance of the older repertoire of dances. Musicians often travel from one temple to the next during the season.

All Buddhist temples celebrate obon in some way. Some temples will host dancing, a few will organize a floating lantern festival, others will have just a service. Especially important is that a family participate in the first bon season after the death of a family member. Though regular participation in bon is not a family's practice, most will adhere to this custom and engage in the festivities of obon. Many will participate annually, reestablishing family ties with the past.

Chusok: **Autumn Night**

The fifteenth of the eighth month of the lunar calendar was once a time for celebration in Asian countries. It is the night of the brightest full moon of the year and marked the beginning of the harvest season.

Koreans refer to this night as *Chusok* or Autumn Night. Moon watching, feasting and a festival atmosphere prevailed as people once enjoyed the first crops of rice and grain and fresh ripened fruits. It was also a time for remembering ancestors, cleaning their grave sites and paying homage and respect much like the Chinese Ch'ing Ming Festival. Chusok was also a time for young people to meet under the light of the moon.

In Hawai'i today, Chusok is commemorated with special family dinners, particularly among newer immigrants to the state. *Song pyun*, a special rice cake, is traditionally made for this occasion. The pink, white and green dumplings are filled with a mixture of sesame seeds and sugar or sweet yellow beans. Pine leaves are placed in the bottom of the steaming vessel to add special flavor to the new rice used to make these cakes. Folk lore among Korean women says that shaping the song pyun prettily would insure a pretty daughter.

Moon Festival

Mid August is also time for the Moon Festival, a Chinese and Vietnamese fete also known as Festival of the Reunion, Mid Autumn Festival or Rewarding the Moon. In Hawai'i it is a time for moon cakes and family gatherings.

The moon is considered a symbol of femininity. Chang O, a beautiful woman who lived in the Hsia Dynasty, stole a pill from her husband that would insure youth and immortality. As she swallowed the pill, she found herself soaring up to the moon where her youth and beauty are preserved forever. But as punishment for her theft, she is on the moon forever.

As in the West, the moon also symbolizes romance. Yueh Lao, the man of the moon, is the universal matchmaker. On this night of the harvest festival he is busy tying destined couples together with invisible red silk thread.

The Festival of the Reunion originated in the Yuan Dynasty when China was invaded by the Mongols in the fourteenth Century. Since the Chinese were under heavy guard, they could not plan a revolution. During the harvest season, the Chinese ate their traditional moon cakes but unknown to their conquering guards, secret messages had been tucked inside to plan their revolution. The revolution was a success and Chinese rule returned.

Moon cakes are still special to the Moon Festival. Made of flour, sugar and shortening, these cakes are filled with coconut, fruit, ham, or sweet bean paste. Salted duck egg,

The Moon Festival celebrated by Chinese and Vietnamese families in August always includes moon cakes, a pastry filled with sweetened beans or other ingredients. These cakes were once used to conceal messages and are available throughout the year in Chinese bakeries.

watermelon seeds and almonds may also be tucked into the center. It is said that eating moon cakes with seeds will bless one with with many children.

While some families make their own moon

cakes, most prefer to buy them from bakeries specializing in Chinese sweets. Moon cakes are abundant around August 15 but are also available throughout the year.

The Chinese believe that when the moon is at its fullest, it is good luck to gaze upon it. The August moon signaled the harvest season; it was a time for farmers to give thanks for the year's bounty. In Hawai'i, families gather to dine and enjoy moon cakes, another legacy of the Chinese immigrants.

Christmas in Hawai'i is celebrated in much the same way as in the rest of the United States. Ethnic diversity is perhaps most noticeable on the dining table where one might find a Christmas dinner of turkey, dressing, cranberries and mashed potatoes served with rice, *sushi, chow mein, kim chee* and *poke*. Gift exchanges, church attendance, caroling and festivity are all part of Christmas in Hawai'i, distinguished by only a couple of ethnic decorative traditions.

A parole, *the Filipino Christmas star, hangs in a Norfolk Pine, the Hawaiian Christmas tree.*

Parole, Filipino Star

The *Parole* is a tradition of the Philippines that can be seen decorating island homes during the Christmas season. Traditionally made of paper, these stars symbolize the star of Bethlehem. In Hawai'i many paroles are three to four feet from point to point and are made of bright colored cloth. Decorated with silver and gold tinsel and lit by light bulbs, the parole is a festive decoration with fond memories for many who came from the Philippines.

Lapinha: Portuguese Nativity

Lapinha is a Christmas tradition for some Portuguese families in Hawai'i, a distinctive decoration of the season in their homes. A tiered nativity scene, the lapinha was brought to the islands by Portuguese immigrants over a hundred years ago. It is set up in different ways, depending on where the original immigrant came from in Portugal and how each family carried on the tradition over succeeding generations.

Figurines of Mary, Joseph, the shepherds and Three Kings are displayed on steps, making up the stable at Bethlehem. The Menino Jesus, the central figure of the lapinha, is usually at the top, dressed in white and made of porcelain or ceramic. Ceramic angels, houses and animals are arranged on the lapinha, too, and the *galos* (rooster), symbol of Portugal, might be present. *Vela* (candles) light up the lapinha, symbolically carrying prayers to heaven.

A lapinha would also feature *trigo* (sprouted wheat) as part of the display. Seven days before Christmas day, wheat seeds are started in small bowls and if properly sprouted, the wheat will grow to an appropriate height by Christmas Eve. Historically, the growth of the trigo meant a good year for the farmer. Today trigo that has grown green and tall, means good fortune will come to the family. If it turns dark and brown and dies, bad luck will prevail.

January 6 is the Feast of the Three Kings, marking the arrival of the Three Kings in Bethlehem. On this day, the lapinha is dismantled and stored for another year. The trigo is planted or buried, marking the conclusion of the Christmas season and the beginning of a new year.

A lapinha, *set up by Elizabeth Jardine of Oʻahu, features figurines from Portugal brought by the first Portuguese immigrants to Hawaiʻi. Bowls of* trigo (wheat) *are sprouted in time for Christmas Eve.*

Bibliography

Adaniya, Ruth, Alice Njus and Margaret Yamate, eds. *Of Andagi and Sanshin: Okinawan Culture in Hawai'i*. Kaneohe, Hawai'i: Hui O Laulima, 1988.

Aero, Rita. *Things Chinese*. New York: Doubleday & Co., 1980.

Aiona, Darrow L. "Hawaiian Funeral." *Social Process in Hawai'i* 22 (1958): 29-32.

Akahoshi, Hidefuni. "Hongwanji in Rural Japan and Cosmopolitan Hawai'i." *Social Process in Hawai'i* 26 (1963): 80-82.

Alailima, Fay C. "The Samoans of Hawai'i." *Social Process in Hawai'i* 29 (1982): 105-12.

Ambrose, Jeanne. "Malassadas Aren't Only Things Portuguese Eat." *Honolulu Star-Bulletin*, August 12, 1987.

Anderson, Robert N., Richard Coller and Rebecca F. Pestano. *Filipinos in Rural Hawai'i*. Honolulu: University of Hawai'i Press, 1984.

Anima, Nid. *Childbirth and Burial: Practices Among Philippine Tribes*. Quezon City: Omar Publications, 1978.

Atipas, Porntipa. "Laotian Refugee Adaptation in Hawai'i." Research paper submitted to the Sociology Dept. as a partial fulfilment of the Ph.D. degree in Sociology, University of Hawai'i, Honolulu, 1987.

Baker, Margaret. *Wedding Customs and Folklore*. New Jersey: Rowman & Littlefield, 1977.

Bazore, Katherine. *Hawaiian and Pacific Foods: A Cookbook of Culinary Customs and Recipes*. New York: Barrows, 1947.

Behrens, June. *Samoans! Festivals and Holidays*. Chicago: Children's Press, 1986.

Berg, Elizabeth. *Family Traditions: Celebrations for Holidays and Everyday*. Pleasantville, New York/Montreal: The Reader's Digest Association Inc., 1992.

Betnam, Mere. "The Family, the Heart of Samoana." Samoan Heritage Series proceedings. College of Continuing Education, State Foundation on Culture and the Arts, The State Council on Samoan Heritage. Honolulu: University of Hawai'i, May 26, 1972.

Bryan, Dawn. *The Art and Etiquette of Gift Giving*. New York: Bantam Books, 1987.

Cariaga, Roman R. "The Filipinos in Hawai'i." Master's Thesis, University of Hawai'i, 1936. Photocopy.

Casal, U. A. *The Five Sacred Festivals of Ancient Japan*. Tokyo: Sophia University in cooperation with C.E. Tuttle Co., 1967.

Cayaban, Ines V. *A Goodly Heritage*. Hong Kong: Gulliver Books, 1981.

Chang, Toy Len. *Chinese Festivals: The Hawaiian Way*. Honolulu, T.L. Chang, 1983.

"Changing Rituals in Chinese Births and Deaths." *Social Process in Hawai'i* 22 (1958): 26-28.

Char, Stephanie Ayers. "Lapinha: A Portuguese Christmas Tradition." *Honolulu*, Vol. 12, December 1977, 41-4.

Chung, May Lee, Dorothy Jim Luke and Margaret Leong Lau, eds. *Traditions for Living: A Booklet of Chinese Customs and Folk Practices in Hawai'i*. Vols. I and II. Honolulu: Associated Chinese University Women, 1979 and 1989.

Coleman, Peter Tali. Keynote Address, Samoan Heritage Series proceedings. College of Continuing Education, State Foundation on Culture and the Arts, The State Council on Samoan Heritage. Honolulu: University of Hawai'i, May 26, 1972.

The Consultation on Common Texts. *A Christian Celebration of Marriage: An Ecumenical Liturgy*. Philadelphia: Fortress Press, 1987.

Corum, Ann Kondo. *Ethnic Foods of Hawai'i*. Honolulu: The Bess Press, 1983.

_____. *Folk Wisdom from Hawai'i*. Honolulu: The Bess Press, 1985.

Cowling, Wendy E. "On Being Tongan: Responses to Concepts of Tradition." Ph.D. Thesis, School of Behavioral Sciences, Macquarie University, Sydney, 1990. Photocopy.

Crane, Paul S. *Korean Patterns*. Seoul: Royal Asiatic Society, 1967.

Crim, Keith, gen. ed., Roger A. Bullard and Larry D. Shinn, assoc. eds. *The Perennial Dictionary of World Religions*. San Francisco: Harper Collins, 1989.

Dang, Lam Sang. "Lunar Time and Festivals in Vietnam." *Journal of Vietnamese Studies* 1 (1990): 45-51.

Daws, Gavan. *Shoal of Time*. Honolulu: University of Hawai'i Press, 1968.

De Francis, John. *Things Japanese in Hawai'i*. Honolulu: University of Hawai'i Press, 1973.

De Garis, Frederic. *We Japanese*, Vol. I. Japan: Fujiya Hotel Ltd., 1934.

De Mente, Boye Lafayette. *Etiquette Guide to Japan*. Tokyo: Charles E. Tuttle Co. Inc. 1990.

Demetrio, Francisco R. and S. J. Radaza. *Dictionary of Philippine Folk Beliefs and Customs II*. Cagayan de Oro City, Philippines: Xavier University, 1970.

Ebisuya, Jan. *A Look at a Hawaiian Baby Luau*. Honolulu: Hawai'i Multicultural Awareness Project, 1977. Filmstrip.

_____. *The Bon Festival in Hawai'i*. Honolulu: Hawai'i Multicultural

Awareness Project, 1979. Filmstrip.
_____. *Chinese New Year in Hawai'i*.
Honolulu: Hawai'i Multicultural
Awareness Project, 1979. Filmstrip.
_____. *Sights and Sounds of a Filipino
Wedding*. Honolulu: Hawai'i
Multicultural Awareness Project, 1977.
Filmstrip.

Ebrey, Patricia Buckley, trans. *Chu Hsi's
Family Rituals: A Twelfth Century Chinese
Manual for the Performance of Cappings,
Weddings, Funerals and Ancestral Rites.*
Princeton, New Jersey: Princeton
University Press, 1991.

Ethnic Resource Center for the Pacific. *A
Legacy of Diversity: Contributions of the
Hawaiians, Chinese, Japanese,
Portuguese,Puerto Ricans, Koreans,
Filipinos and Samoans in Hawai'i.*
Honolulu: University of Hawai'i, 1975.

Favorite Island Cookery. Honolulu: Honpa
Hongwanji Buddhist Temple, 1973.

Favorite Island Cookery Book III.
Honolulu: Honpa Hongwanji Buddhist
Temple, 1979.

Felix, John Henry and Peter F. Senecal. *The
Portuguese in Hawai'i Centennial Edition.*
Honolulu, 1978.

Fiesta Islands. *The Fiesta Islands: Festivals of
the Philippines.* Philippines: National
Media Production Center, 1970.

Freitas, J. F. *Portuguese Hawaiian Memories.*
Honolulu, 1930.

Gallagher, Charles F. *Hawai'i and Its Gods.*
New York: Weatherhill/Kapa, 1975.

Gaster, Theodor. *New Year: Its History,
Customs and Superstitions.* New York:
Abelard Schuman, 1955.

Grattan, F.J.H. *An Introduction to Samoan
Custom.* 1948. Reprint. Papakura, New
Zealand: R. McMillan, 1985.

Green, Laura C. and Martha Warren
Beckwith. "Hawaiian Household
Customs." *American Anthropologist* 30,
January-March 1928.

Gutmanis, June. *Na Pule Kahiko: Ancient
Hawaiian Prayers.* Honolulu: Editions
Limited, 1983.

Ha, Tae-Hung. *Guide to Korean Culture.*
Seoul: Yonsei University Press, 1968.

Handy, E.S. Craighill and Mary Kawena
Pukui. *The Polynesian Family System in
Ka'u Hawai'i.* Tokyo, Japan: Charles E.
Tuttle Co., 1972.

Harada, Wayne. "For the New Year." *The
Honolulu Advertiser*, Dec. 18, 1992.

Hawai'i Herald. Tenth Anniversary Issue.
Vol. II, No.10. Honolulu, May 18, 1990.

Hazama, Dorothy Ochiai and Jane Okamoto
Komeiji. *Okage sama de: The Japanese in
Hawai'i, 1885-1985.* Honolulu: Bess Press,
1987.

Holmes, Lowell D. *Samoan Village.* New York:
Holt, Rinehart & Winston, 1974.

Hu, William C. *Chinese New Year: Fact and
Folklore.* Michigan: Ars Ceramica, Ltd.
1991.

Hung, Chen Kuo. *We Call Our Treasure Tan
Heung Shan.* Honolulu: Bank of Hawai'i,
1989.

Huynh, Dinh Te. "Introduction to Viet-
namese Culture." In *Introduction to the
Indochinese and Their Cultures.* San Diego:
Multifunctional Resource Center, San
Diego State University, 1989.

Hyoe, Murakami and Edward G.
Seidensticker. *Guides to Japanese Culture.*
Japan: Japan Culture Institute, 1977.

Japan-America Society of Honolulu in
cooperation with The East West Center,
The Center for Japanese Studies,
University of Hawai'i. *Roots of Japanese
Behavior.* Proceedings of the symposium,
East-West Center, October 13-14, 1989.

Japan Culture Institute. *A Hundred Things
Japanese.* Japan: Japan Culture Institute,
1975.

Joya, Mock. *Things Japanese.* Japan: The
Japan Times Ltd., 1985.

Ka'ano'i, Patrick. *The Need for Hawai'i: A
Guide to Hawaiian Cultural and Kahuna
Values.* Honolulu, 1992.

Kanahele, Dr. George S. ed. *"Ho'okipa" in
Hawaiian Values, Series 1.* Project Waiaha.

Kimura, Sueko H. "Japanese Funeral
Practices in Pahoa." *Social Process in

Hawai'i* 22 (1958): 21-25.

Lagerwey, John. *Taoist Ritual in Chinese
Society and History.* New York: Macmillan
Publishing Co., 1987.

Language Research Center, Brigham Young
University. *Kingdom of Tonga.* Provo,
Utah: Brigham Young University, 1980.

Lind, Andrew W. *Hawai'i's People.*
Honolulu: University of Hawai'i Press,
1980.

Lipman, Victor. "In Another Country: The
Samoans in Hawai'i." *Honolulu*, Vol. 14,
January 1980, 68-78.

Liu, Da. *The Tao and Chinese Culture.* New
York: Schocken Books, 1979.

Martin, Judith. *Miss Manners Guide for the
Turn-of-the-Milennium.* New York: Pharos
Books, 1989.

McDermott, John F. Jr. et. al. *People and
Cultures of Hawai'i: A Psychocultural
Profile.* Honolulu: University of Hawai'i
Press, 1980.

Mehta, Julie. *Christmas in Hawai'i.* Honolulu:
Mutual Publishing, 1991.

Morgan, Harry T. *Chinese Symbols and
Superstitions.* California: P.D. and Ione
Perkins, 1942.

Morse, Harold. "Feast of the Holy Ghost
Coming Up." *Honolulu Star Bulletin*,
June 27, 1980.

Mulholland, John F. *Hawai'i's Religions.*
Tokyo: Charles E. Tuttle Co., 1970.

Nakajima, Bun. *Japanese Etiquette.* 1955. 2d
ed. Tokyo: Japan Travel Bureau, 1957.

Nguyen, Tim R. *Chung Minh Tim Hieu:
We Want to Know.* Honolulu: A'o Like
Project, 1983.

Nguyen, Dinh Te. "The Vietnamese Family
Moral Code." *Journal of Vietnamese Studies*
1 (1990): 32-36.

Nordyke, Eleanor C. *The Peopling of Hawai'i.*
Honolulu: University of Hawai'i Press,
1989.

Office of Hawaiian Affairs. *Ho'okipa:
Hawaiian Hospitality.* Honolulu: Office of
Hawaiian Affairs, 1988.

Ogawa, Dennis. *Jan Ken Po: The World of
Hawai'i's Japanese Americans.* Honolulu:

Japanese American Research Center, Honolulu Japanese Chamber of Commerce, 1973.

Ogawa, Dennis and Glen Grant. *Hawai'i's Yakudoshi Guide Book*. Honolulu: Nippon Golden Network and Times Supermarket, 1990.

Omori, Gary. "Samoans in Hawai'i: Culture in Conflict." In *The Samoans in Hawai'i: A Resource Guide*. Honolulu: Ethnic Research and Resource Center, University of Hawai'i, February 1973.

Ono, Dr. Sokyo. *Shinto: The Kami Way*. Tokyo: Charles E. Tuttle Co. 1962.

Pang, Duane J.L. *The "K'ai Kuang" Lion Ceremony*. Honolulu: Hawai'i Chinese History Center, 1976.

Pukui, Mary Kawena, E. W. Haertig, M.D. and Catherine A. Lee. *Nana I Ke Kumu (Look to the Source)*. Vol. I and II. Honolulu: Queen Liliuokalani Children's Center, 1972.

Reed, Le'aeno T. W. "The Village, the Guardian of Samoa." Samoan Heritage Series proceedings. College of Continuing Education, State Foundation on Culture and the Arts, The State Council on Samoan Heritage. Honolulu: University of Hawai'i, May 26, 1972.

Rho, Marguerite, ed. "Portuguese Centennial" in *Ampersand*, Vol. XII, No. 3, pp 22-7. Honolulu: Alexander and Baldwin Inc.

Roces, Alfredo and Grace. *Culture Shock! Philippines*. 3d ed. Portland, Oregon: Graphic Arts Center Publishing Co., 1992.

Rutt, Richard. *Korean Works and Days*. Korea: Korea Branch, Royal Asiatic Society, 1964.

Ryan, Paul and Noel Murchie. "Step into Hawai'i's Portuguese Past." *The Honolulu Advertiser*, April 4, 1986.

Sakihara, Mitsugu. *Rituals and Food in Okinawa*. Photocopy of paper.

Saso, Michael. *Blue Dragon White Tiger: Taoist Rites of Passage*. Washington, D.C.: The Taoist Center, dist. by University of

Hawai'i Press, 1990.

Sawyer, Gene. *Celebrations: Asia and the Pacific*. Honolulu: Friends of the East-West Center, 1978.

75th Anniversary of Korean Immigration to Hawai'i, 1903-1978. Honolulu: 75th Anniversary of Korean Immigration to Hawai'i Committee, 1978.

Simonds, Nina. "Chinese New Year." Los Angeles Times Syndicate, *The Honolulu Advertiser*, January 20, 1993.

Stephenson, Larry K. and Amy A. Miyashiro. "Rural Urban Contrasts of Kumiai's in Hawai'i." *Social Process in Hawai'i* 27 (1979): 76-85.

Steubel C. and Bro. Herman, adaptors. *Tala o le Vavau: The Myths, Legends and Customs of Old Samoa*. New Zealand: Polynesian Press, 1987.

Tava, Rerioterai and Moses K. Keale Sr. *Niihau: The Traditions of an Hawaiian Island*. Honolulu: Mutual Publishing Co., 1989.

Thom, Wah Chan. *The Story of Mānoa Chinese Cemetery*. Honolulu: Lin Yee Chung Association, 1985.

Tom, Dr. K. S. *Echoes from Old China: Life, Legends and Lore of the Middle Kingdom*. Honolulu: Hawai'i Chinese History Center, dist. by University of Hawai'i Press, 1939.

Tseng, Wen-Shing, John F. McDermott, Jr., and Thomas W. Maretzki, eds. *People and Cultures in Hawai'i: An Introduction for Mental Health Workers*. Transcultural Psychiatry Committee, Department of Psychiatry, University of Hawai'i School of Medicine. Honolulu: University of Hawai'i, 1974.

Tuleja, Tad. *Curious Customs*. New York: Harmony Books, 1987.

Van Zile, Judy. "Japanese Bon Dance and Hawai'i: Mutual Influences." *Social Process in Hawai'i* 30 (1983): 49-56.

Verploegen, Hildegaard. "Bad Dough is Best." *The Honolulu Advertiser*, July 26, 1973.

Votti, Vicky. "Wedding Gifts: The Toaster Trap." *The Honolulu Advertiser*,

August 8, 1989.

Yamaguchi, H.S.K. *We Japanese, Book II*. Japan: Fujiya Hotel Ltd., 1937.

Yamamoto, George K. "The Japanese." *Social Process in Hawai'i* 29 (1982): 60-69.

Young Women's Christian Association of Tokyo, World Fellowship Committee. *Japanese Etiquette: An Introduction*. 1955, 23d ptg. Japan: Charles E. Tuttle Co., 1979.

Interviews

Numerous conversations and interviews transpired over the course of several months as the author gained insight, information and facts about the cultural practices and customs observed by many families in Hawai'i today. The author acknowledges the following for their time, interest, enthusiasm and willingness to share their experiences during these discussions conducted in person or over the telephone:

Rev. Russell Becker, Catholic Diocese of Hawai'i, June 22, 1993

Bea Bonilla, June 24, 1993

James Brown, Sheraton-Waikiki Catering

Dr. Leon H. Bruno, Lyman Museum, Hilo, May 6, 1993

Barbara Bulatao, June 24, 1993

Buddy Bullard, Borthwick Mortuary, Maui, May 11, 1993

Laurabelle Butler, June 22, 1993

Patrick V. Caires, Homelani Memorial Park, Hilo, May 5, 1993

Hoa Caluya, June 2, 1993

Hilda Cannon, June 24, 1993

Richard Cheung, July 21, 1993

Bill and Rose Chong, February 23, 1993

Bob and Lily Chow, May 5, 1993

Albert Q. M. Chun, June 25, 1993

Bob Clarke

S. Rick Crump, Hawaiian Memorial Park, O'ahu, March 17, 1993

Marcelina Domingo
Ismael I. Eustaquio, March 16, 1993
Bennette M. Evangelista, June 18, 1993
Rev. Langi Fine, First United Methodist
Church, April 28, 1993
Burt Freeland, Borthwick Mortuary, Maui,
May 11, 1993
Rev. Yoshiaki Fujitani, Hongwanji Mission,
April 6, 1993
Olympia Furtado
Pulefano Galea'i, Polynesian Cultural
Center, July 13, 1993
Howard and Shirley Han
Salome Han
Fay Haverly
Hong Min and Violet Hee, June 25, 1993
Richard and Eleanor Henderson,
May 5, 1993
Charlaine Higashi, July 22, 1993
Steven Hinck, Hilton Hawaiian Village
Hotel Catering
Moi Lee Hong, March 16, 1993
Rev. Dogen Hosokawa, Chozen-Ji
International Zen Dojo, June 15, 1993
David S. Ikawa, May 5, 1993
Martha Ishihara
Elizabeth Jardine
Stephanie Jardine
Tuti Kanahele, April 26, 1993
Unaloto Kioa, July 13, 1993
Pauline Koreyasu
Chieko Kudaishi, July 12, 1993
Stanley S. Kutsunai, Dodo Mortuary Inc.,
Hilo, May 5, 1993
Bea Lau, May 6, 1993
Rev. Jesse H. Lee, Korean Christian Church,
April 28, 1993
Sam and Jackie Lee, February 17, 1993
Rev. Samuel Lee, April 5, 1993
Arlene Lum, April 28, 1993
Mariko Lyons, April 14, 1993
Lynn Manuel, May 6, 1993
Kathy Matayoshi, May 2, 1993
Lou Michinaka, May 13, 1993
Thanh Mougeot, June 16, 1993
Jean Nakayama, May 11, 1993
Mau Vinh Ngo, June 16, 1993
Dennis Ogawa, April 12, 1993

Michael A. Oh, Mililani Memorial Park,
Oah'u, April 13, 1993
Rev. Akihiro Okada, Daijingu Temple of
Hawai'i, May 1, 1993
Precila Peros, May 14, 1993
Jocelyn Perreira, May 14, 1993
Pathana Rattanasamay, July 19, 1993
Sengdao Rattanasamay, April 29, 1993
Mary Riveira, April 28, 1993
Bonnie Rodriguez, Diamond Head Mortuary,
O'ahu, April 12, 1993
Brent A. Schwenke, July 22, 1993
Eldeen Scott, June 25, 1993
Jean K. Seki, April 16, 1993
Evelyn Shon, April 6, 1993
Beverly Takayama, June 23, 1993
Barbara Tanaka, May 14, 1993
Mieko Tanouye, May 17, 1993
Gladys Tashiro, June 24, 1993
Dr. Francis Terada, June 23, 1993
Regina Ting, May 13, 1993
Emme Tomimbang, April 19, 1993
Derwin S. Tsutsui, Hosoi Garden Mortuary,
Oahu, March 26, 1993
Jerry Vandermark, Borthwick Mortuary,
Oah'u, May 3, 1993
Leonora Vidinha, June 24, 1993
Betty Wo, June 21, 1993
Polly Wo, May 28, 1993
Laurie Wong, March 16, 1993
Aina White, May 6, 1993
Gregg and Ruthann Yamanaka
Jane Yamanaka, March 23, 1993
Fran Yamamoto, May 13, 1993
Dong Sook Yoo, July 8, 1993

In addition to the many people who provided
me with their time, anecdotes and personal
histories, the author gratefully acknowledges
the following people and organizations who
provided information, materials and
references: Tanya Alston; Sam and Lily
Domingo; Ann Hayashi, Japanese Cultural
Center; Dorothy Hoe; The Immigrant
Center; Carol Nakamoto; Hyatt Regency
Waikiki Catering; Portuguese Heritage
Council; Waipahu Plantation Village.

109

The Author, The Photographer and The Artist

Joan Clarke is the daughter of Korean immigrants, born and raised in Hawai'i. She is a graduate of Kailua High School and the University of Washington. Following a successful career in retailing she has "retired" to become a free lance writer.

Mike Uno has been a professional free lance photographer for over twenty years. He is *sansei* (third generation Hawaii born Japanese), a graduate of Kalani High School and DePauw University, Indiana.

Susanne Yuu is a graduate of Waipahu High School and studied art at the University of Hawaii. She is also sansei and has been a free lance graphic artist for twenty five years.